Crossway Bible Guide

Series Editors: Ian Coffey (NT), Stephen Gaukroger (OT)
Old Testament Editor: Stephen Dray

Also in this series

Acts: Stephen Gaukroger

Dedicated to the memory of my father,
Albert Harry Dray (1927-1992), who died during the
final preparations on this book and whose life was
characterised as that of one 'free to serve'.

Exodus: Crossway Bible Guide

Free to Serve

Stephen Dray

Crossway Books
Nottingham

ISBN 1 85684 050-6

Unless otherwise stated, Scripture quotations in this publication are
from the Holy Bible, New International Version. Copyright © 1973,
1978, 1984 International Bible Society. Published in Great Britain by
Hodder & Stoughton Ltd.

Typeset by Saxon Graphics Ltd, Derby
Printed in Great Britain for Crossway Books, Norton Street,
Nottingham NG7 3HR by Cox & Wyman Ltd, Reading, Berkshire

Contents

Illustrations

Map

Crossway Bible Guides

Series Editors' Introduction

Today, the groups of people who meet together to study the Bible appear to be a booming leisure-time activity in many parts of the world. In the United Kingdom alone, over one million people each week meet in home Bible-study groups.

This series has been designed to help such groups – and, in particular, those who lead them. We are also aware of the needs of those who preach and teach to larger groups as well as the hard-pressed student, all of whom often look for a commentary that gives a concise summary and lively application of a particular passage. We have tried to keep three clear aims in our sights:

1. To explain and apply the message of the Bible in non-technical language.
2. To encourage discussion, prayer and action on what the Bible teaches.
3. To enlist authors who are in the business of teaching the Bible to others and are doing it well.

All of us engaged in the project believe that the Bible is the Word of God – given to us in order that people might discover Him and His purposes for our lives. We believe that the 66 books which go to make up the Bible although written by different people, in different places, at different times, through different circumstances, have a single unifying theme: that theme is Salvation.

All of us hope that the books in this series will help people get a grip on the message of the Bible. But most important of all, we pray that the Bible will get a grip on you as a result!

Ian Coffey   Stephen Gaukroger
Series Editors

Note to readers

In our Bible Guides, we have developed special symbols, to make things easier to follow. Every passage therefore has an opening section which is

the passage in a nutshell

The main section is the one that *makes sense of the passage.* This is marked with a blackboard.

Questions: Every passage also has special questions for group and personal study in a box after the main section. Some questions are addressed to us as individuals, some speak to us as members of our church or home group, while others concern us as members of God's people worldwide.

Some passages, however, require an extra amount of explanation, and we have put these sections into two categories. The first kind gives additional background material that help us understand something complex. For example, if we study the Gospels, it helps us to know who the Pharisees were, so that we can see more easily why they related to Jesus in the way they did. These technical sections are marked with an open book.

Finally, some passages have important doctrines contained in them, which we need to study in more depth if we are to grow as Christians. Special sections that explain them to us in greater detail are marked with a mortar board.

Waiting on tiptoe

Why should I read Exodus?

Every nation and people of the world have great and exciting stories of the exploits of their founders and ancestors. In ancient books and around camp fires these stories are told and retold; stories to captivate the listeners with tales of great battles, dramatic interventions by the gods, the conquest of good over evil and the victory of one man or a small group over overwhelming opposition.

Few such stories, however, can have aroused such interest as the true stories of the book of Exodus. Children are entranced by the story of Moses' birth, the ten plagues and the journey through the Red Sea. Film-makers have found in these tales material for dramatic epics. Oppressed people, even today, have found that they can identify with the Israelites and long, with them, to be released from their burdens. Especially in South America and Africa the Exodus stories continue to arouse powerful emotions and sympathy.

However, all this interest has often been accompanied by ignorance of the reasons which led to the story being told. Often, those who have sought to find a meaning in the Exodus stories have failed to understand them correctly. As we study these chapters we will try to show how they should be understood and emphasise that these tales of long ago are, truly, *our* story too.

The Story so far
The book of Exodus is part of a larger story: the Bible story. As a result of this we will only understand its message clearly if we remember what has already happened in the Bible history.

The book of Genesis which comes before Exodus can be divided into three unequal parts:

I   In the first two chapters God's creation of the world is described.
II   This is followed in chapters 3–11 by the sad tale of mankind's fall into sin.
III   In the remainder of the book, God takes one man and his descendants and promises that through them He will bring salvation into the world.

As we understand Genesis better, so we will also enjoy reading Exodus even more.

The Message of Genesis

I. Creation (chapters 1 and 2)

These chapters describe God's creation of everything and His verdict that it was perfect (1:31). We are then told that God placed the first man and his wife, Adam and Eve, in the most delightful part of that perfect world. There they were able to enjoy without any hindrance both God Himself and the entire created world. By doing this God wanted to arouse Adam and Eve's love for Him so that He might enjoy their friendship and that they might experience His blessing.

II. Fall (chapters 3–11)

The beginning of sin Sadly, tragedy followed. Rather than be grateful for all that God had provided for them, Adam and his wife became resentful that He had placed one small prohibition upon them in order to test their love for Him. Selfishly, they turned their backs on God's love and disobeyed Him. The results were immediate. In these chapters the consequences of that initial sin are vividly described. Adam and Eve now experienced God as one to be feared: one from whom they were separated (3:8). They were told, and quickly discovered, that a hostility had sprung up between them (3:12,16) and that the world itself had turned against them (3:17-19). They must now die (3:19).

The spread of sin The disease of sin is then seen to spread to all of their descendants. One of their own sons, Cain, develops such a hatred of his brother that he committed murder (4:8). Cain's own descendants include the murderous and bloodthirsty Lamech (4:23,24). Eventually, the whole of the ancient world is described as completely enslaved to sin:

'every inclination of the thoughts of men and women were only evil all the time' (6:5).

The consequence of sin This is then vividly described in chapters 6–11. The judgment of God against all sin is set forth in the story of the Flood (chapters 7 and 8). Even the fact that God delivered Noah and his family only serves to emphasise the serious consequences which result from sin in the world. For though Noah was saved from the world of sinners, sin itself had not left even righteous Noah (9:20-27). Soon the world was just as sinful as it was before the Flood (chapter 11). Mankind is seen to be enslaved to sin and without hope of escape.

An old answer to a modern problem At this point, we need to summarise some of the lessons of these early chapters in the Bible. They begin by teaching us that when God made the world it was perfect and free from sin and death. However, in the chapters which follow the reasons are given which explain why we do not experience the world in such a way today: sin and death have entered into God's perfect world. This happened when Adam and his wife rebelled against God. The results of sin in the world are then spelt out for us in tragic detail.

Thus:

Sin has extended to all mankind In the New Testament Paul can say: 'Sin entered the world through one man...and in this way death (which is the result of sin) came to all men' (Rom 5:12). Understanding how this has happened is not easy. However, we can say that such a verdict does explain the world as we know and experience it.

Sin has affected every part of man The early chapters of Genesis illustrate that Paul was quite right to say that the world is full of 'immorality, impurity, debauchery, idolatry, witchcraft, hatred, jealousy, fits of rage, selfishness' (Gal 5:19-21). Thus we see that the actions of men and women are affected by sin.

Moreover, both the Bible as a whole, and the early chapters of Genesis in particular, emphasise that the problem of sin is serious. Genesis 6:5, which was quoted above, shows us that the minds and the understandings of all men are affected by sin so that 'every inclination of the thoughts of man's heart was only evil all the time'. The result of this is well expressed by Paul in Romans 1:24 when he says: 'God gave men over to the sinful desires of their hearts'. In this way Paul teaches that even the desires and emotions of men are governed by sin.

Most serious of all, however, is the fact that the wills and hearts of men are infected by sin. Jesus realised this when He said: 'Everyone who sins is a slave of sin' (John 8:34). A slave can only serve his master. A sinner can only serve sin. And Paul says: '*all* have sinned' (Rom 3:23). Genesis 6:5 teaches the same truth when it speaks of the thoughts of the human *heart* because the heart in the Bible is the centre of human nature. Sin is like a disease damaging every part of the nature of every person on earth.

Sin has affected the whole created order

Adam was told in Genesis 3:17, 'the ground is cursed because of you'. Paul could echo the same truth when he said: 'the creation was made subject to frustration' (Rom 8:20). The burden of work and toil is the result of God's curse on the earth. Before we go any further we ought to notice the consequences of all this for us.

i While we can and do accomplish 'good' things, yet we can never achieve lifelong perfection of our inner thoughts and our outward actions. But this is what is necessary if we are ever to become the friends of God again.

ii We are unable to save ourselves from the predicament sin has brought us into. Affected by sin in every part, we have neither the will nor the strength to save ourselves.

iii Unable to do God's will and incapable of even hearing His voice clearly, we are under His judgment. So Paul taught that: 'judgment followed one sin and brought condemnation' (Rom 5:16).

iv In ignorant fear of God, we try to make ourselves our own masters. Paul again said: 'He opposes and exalts himself over everything that is called God' (2 Thess 2:4). We set our own standards and then claim that God ought to accept us, excusing our sinful ways. We do what we want and then demand the favour of God!

v Man is now turned against man. The world is full of conflict, exploitation and misunderstanding which sours even the best of relationships. Thus when Adam turned against Eve and Cain against Abel (Gen 3:12; 4:8) they were only the first of all the quarrelling people in the world.

vi We are now incapable of judging ourselves properly. Thus inner conflict, doubts, fears and restlessness are the result. The prophet Isaiah once said: 'The wicked are like the tossing sea which cannot rest... There is no peace...for the wicked' (Isa 57:20). We sometimes meet people who can think only of themselves. At other times we come to know people who seem to despise themselves. These are two of the ways in which sin is so often experienced by men and women.

vii We can no longer exercise our God-given authority over the creation properly. The result is seen in the selfish hoarding of God's gifts by some which create a desperate lack for others and in the exploitation of those gifts by many of us in such a way as leads to pollution of our own world. viii Finally, we are now subject to death. However, in the face of its inevitability we try to cling onto the passing pleasures of life.

This tragic and inescapable conclusion is thus set before us in chapters 3–11 of Genesis.

III. Promise (chapters 12–50)

Then God intervened! Indeed, at the moment of the first sin God had promised to do something about the problem. God said that one day someone would be born who would put the whole sinful world right by breaking the power of sin (3:15). In chapter 12 God takes one man, Abraham, and then his descendants and says again that this earlier promise will be fulfilled through them. One day, the whole world will be blessed through them! To achieve this, God promised Abraham that his descendants would become a great nation who would live in Palestine and be a blessing to the world. This promise is repeated throughout the last 38 chapters of Genesis rather like a chorus: first to Abraham (12:1–3; 15:1–17; 17:4–7; 22:15–18) then to Isaac his son (28:13,14) and, finally, to Jacob (35:9–12).

At the end of Genesis this promise is eagerly awaited. Though Abraham's descendants were now living in Egypt (as God had forecast, (15:13)), Jacob and Joseph looked forward to the time when God would act and fulfil His promises (47:30; 48:21-22).

Rather as children will stand on tiptoe to look over a wall to see what is on the other side, so the book of Genesis encourages us to stand on tiptoe too, and ask the question: 'When will God fulfil His promises and begin to save this world from sin?'

At this point the book of Exodus begins!

Exodus 1:1–7

Our blindness to God's blessings

God often begins a great work in a small way. The Israelites were only few when they entered Egypt but God blessed them and they rapidly began to grow in number. Sadly, however, they seem to have lost their vision.

The book of Genesis ends by looking forward. The book of Exodus, by contrast, marks the new start in the story of God's promises by looking back: recalling the entry of Jacob's family into Egypt (vv.1-4). A vital fact is then stressed. When Abraham's descendants entered Egypt (which was the greatest power in the ancient world), they were only seventy in number (v.5).

However, from such small beginnings God began to work. As verses 6 and 7 tell us, God quickly began to fulfil His promises in the remarkable growth of the people of Israel. Soon their numbers are such that Egypt is not big enough to contain them; they need a land of their own! Later this amazing fact will become even more apparent (12:37). However, here we are simply told the basic fact but in language which echoes God's promises in Genesis 12:2; 17:6 and 35:11.

Perhaps even more remarkable is the fact that there is a more distant echo from verses 6 and 7 back to Genesis 1:28. God had commanded perfect man and woman to multiply and fill the earth. In Egypt, as their numbers grew and grew, Israel experienced such blessing as was unheard of since the entrance of sin into the world. They are described as if they were enjoying the experience of a world without the effects of sin!

Such blessings might have been expected to stir up the Israelites to look with anticipation for the further fulfilment of God's promises. Sadly, however, the attitude which Jacob and Joseph showed (Gen 47:30; 48:21–22) is absent. Not until circumstances force them to, do the Israelites recapture the desire which marked their ancestors and rediscover their calling to be a blessing to the world. It is easy, too, for Christians to enjoy the salvation blessings of God themselves and yet lose sight of their responsibility to bring that salvation blessing to those around them who know nothing of salvation. Sometimes God has to remove the experience of His blessing from Christians, as He did with Israel in Egypt, before Christians are ready to meet their God-given responsibilities towards their neighbours and their world.

Questions

1. *How does this passage show us the purpose of God for His own people. Why has God gathered His people together in a worldwide church?*

2. *God had blessed Israel so that they might become a blessing to others. Is my church selfish in the way we seek and enjoy God's blessings and gifts? How can we learn to view God's gifts as given so that we can share them with others? What gifts has He given us and how may we use them for the sake of others, especially non-Christians?*

3. *The Israelites failed to realise the blessings which God had given them. Do I, perhaps, fail to realise what God has done for me? Am I as aware as I should be of all that God has done to save me? Do I recognise the daily blessings He gives me and do I notice the answers to my prayers? In what other ways do I fail to see what He has done and is doing for me?*

Exodus 1:8–22

Our battles belong to the Lord

The growth of Israel is seen as a threat by the king of Egypt. However, the Lord our God is greater than any human power and the king's purposes are frustrated at every turn.

God had commanded Adam to 'subdue the earth' (Gen 1:28). However, usually the result of sin entering the world has meant that men and women try to subdue one another! Thus the world is full of people who eagerly seek power over others and who will do everything they can to hold on to power. The history of the world is full of examples of those who have gained, or even usurped, power and have then been haunted by the possibility that others may overthrow them. Usually they have dealt with all real or supposed threats against them with great harshness and violence. It was so in Egypt for God's people. A new Pharaoh saw the people of Israel as a threat to his power and rule (vv.8-10). He determined to act against them.

We can easily understand Pharaoh's anxiety at the increasing numbers of the Israelites. His own father had usurped the throne of Egypt and, in the early years of his reign, he was probably still trying to establish his authority (on this see 'The Pharaoh who oppressed the Israelites'). The threat of the Israelites was doubtless seen as very great indeed. Pharaoh decided, as many in his situation have done since, to adopt a policy of deliberate and ruthless repression. His first attempt is described in verses 11-14 where he tried to keep the Israelites so busy making bricks that they could have little energy left to plot against the king. His success was, however, threatened by the continued blessing of God on the people (v.12). The greater the oppression by Pharaoh, the more the Israelites grew in numbers! Though the one who is flexing his muscles was the greatest power on earth in the ancient world, we are already assured that the battle is an uneven one. The question is not who will win the contest but how it will be achieved!

The king immediately decided to resort to more drastic measures (vv.15-21) by attempting to have all Israelite baby boys killed at birth. This policy was vicious but also understandable. As the surviving girls grew up they would be forced to find husbands among the Egyptians. In this way the Israelites as a distinct nation would be completely eliminated. But this also failed because Pharaoh was unable to gain the co-operation of the midwives, who refused to become murderers of Israelite boys.

Possibly the king believed his power would be enough to intimidate these midwives. However, once again, Pharaoh met a greater force than his own because these midwives 'feared God'. The midwives said that the Hebrew women gave birth before the midwives arrived. This excuse may have been partly true. The Israelite women were probably more physically active than Egyptian women and this may have made child-bearing easier. It is also possible that the curse of Genesis 3:16 was partly removed from the Israelite women – a fact which may explain the large increase in the number of births. Sadly, it is difficult to avoid the conclusion that the midwives did lie. The king, however, could not punish them because that would have exposed his cruel plan.

God rewarded the midwives (v.21). Perhaps surprisingly, there is far less condemnation of lying in the Old Testament than Christians might expect. This is probably because the Old Testament is only too aware of the plight of the helpless person brought face to face with those authorities who have rejected all mercy and morality. To be killed for the sake of the truth is a noble ideal but all too often the skilled interrogator knows how to frame his questions so that even silence can betray and condemn others to death. Thus, if Christians in similar situations today have sometimes lied, we should be wary of condemning them.

Finally, Pharaoh issued his last decree (v.22). Every male baby had to be thrown into the Nile. This great river was regarded by the Egyptians as one of the most powerful gods in ancient Egypt. It is probable, therefore, that the king had a religious reason for acting in the way that he did: 'Let the god of the Nile decide what to do with these troublesome Israelites!' But God had another idea, and used the river to preserve Moses!

These verses describe the attempt of one king (though perhaps the most powerful man in the ancient world) to eliminate the Israelites and at the same time destroy the purposes and promises of God. However, there is another theme illustrated in this story: the King of kings was also active! God was concerned to preserve His people. He also allowed much suffering and tragedy. He did this then, and sometimes does the same today, to arouse the people of God from their dependence on the comforts provided by Him, and to awaken them to their calling to be witnesses to Him.

Questions
1. *When I consider my own circumstances, that of my country, and world, how do I view the difficulties and obstacles? What reasons do I have to be confident concerning the purposes of God for both me and the world?*
2. *The church of God often goes through hard times. What lessons can be learnt from this passage which might encourage my own fellowship?*
3. *When in difficulty and trouble, how do I understand what is happening to me? What do these verses teach which will enable me to see what is happening to me?*

The Pharaoh who oppressed the Israelites

We cannot be sure which Pharaoh of ancient Egypt is mentioned here since only his official title is given. However, according to 1 Kings 6:1 the temple of Solomon, begun in the fourth year of his reign, was started 480 years after the Exodus. From our knowledge of ancient history we know that Solomon began to build in 966 B.C. Though many have doubted whether the figure 480 is to be understood literally, it does seem increasingly likely that it is an accurate figure. This would give the date of the exodus as about 1445 B.C. which was during the reign of Amenhotep II. Since the events described in Exodus 1 occurred at least 80 years before the exodus (for Moses was 80 at that time, see 7:7), a date of about 1525 B.C. would seem appropriate to the events of Exodus 1. We can probably therefore identify the Pharaoh who oppressed the Israelites with Amenhotep I. This is the view I agree with. However, there are still many who argue for a later date and further details of such views may be found in Bible Dictionaries.

Exodus 2:1–10

God begins His great work through faithful 'unknown' people

Silently, so silently God begins to work through a humble husband, wife and a little girl. It is often through faithful obedience among the least of God's people that mighty works are started!

The situation described at the end of chapter 1 was desperate indeed for the Israelites. They stood in imminent danger of extinction. The god-king of Egypt and the Nile-god were ready to use all their power and resources to eliminate the people of God once and for all. More seriously still, the very promises of God were under threat. How could such disaster be averted?

Perhaps surprisingly, the answer begins to unfold as we are introduced to a domestic scene in the family of one of the obscure and hated Israelite slaves. Most of us are never likely to become great leaders of God's people. As a result of this we tend to think that it is not so important for us to be faithful to God or trust Him. After all, what difference can our obedience or even disobedience make to the purposes of God?

The Bible does not allow us to think like this. It describes in the Book of Ruth the faithfulness of a humble farmer Boaz and his wife Ruth in a small village community in Palestine. They became great-grandparents of David who was one of the two greatest leaders of Israel. Moreover, David himself was an ancestor of the Saviour of the world! What worldwide blessings sprang from the obedience of Boaz and Ruth!

A similar situation is described in the early verses of Exodus 2. In the face of great disaster we are introduced to Amram and Jochebed. Their names are given in 6:20 but are omitted here, probably to emphasise their obscurity. At the time of Pharaoh's decree (1:22) Jochebed had a son (v.2). Perhaps the fact that she recognised him to be a 'fine' child suggests that she suspected that this helpless baby would one day have a great role to play. Certainly, it suggests that she was looking for God to fulfil His promises. She obeyed the king but entrusted her little child to the God who had made the Nile (v.3). It is possible that she deliberately left the child near a place where it was known that Pharaoh's daughter bathed (v.5) and this might explain why the little boy's sister was stationed nearby to watch (v.4). If so, her faith was soon rewarded! Pharaoh's daughter found and adopted the child and entrusted the baby to its mother as a nurse. The name given to the child, Moses (v.10), must have increased Jochebed's hopes. She would have seen in his name ('drawn out') not only a reference to how he was found but also encouragement to believe he would 'draw out' the people of God from Egypt and lead them to the land of promise.

The story which follows shows very clearly the results of Jochebed's faith. Moses became the one Israelite to equal David in the history of Israel. What a challenge this is to us to be faithful where we are.

We are not told exactly when Pharaoh's cruel decree ended. It has been suggested that the compassion of the princess was shared by others and that this persuaded Pharaoh to change his policy. Possibly, Moses' deliverance was seen as a rejection by the Nile-god of such cruel practices. Certainly, we can see this story as describing the victory of the Nile's Creator over the river's claims to deity: a victory which would shortly be won again!

Here we see God at work; silently at first, equipping Moses with those skills and abilities which will later be required of him and will help make him the great deliverer of God's people. It will nevertheless be nearly 80 years before God is ready to act. God's time-scale is rarely ours and we can often be deceived into thinking that He is inactive, even unconcerned. Yet God is working all the time, unseen by us. These verses remind us of this great truth which often lies behind our present trials and difficulties.

Questions

1. When Christians are faced by the mighty powers that so often oppose God and His ways, how might they respond in the light of this passage?

2. God's plan to save Israel began with a faithful and visionary woman who did what she could in her own small way. None of us are useless in God's service. What might we do for God?

3. God often works slowly and silently to accomplish his plans. Have I the faith to believe He is at work in me and my situation even when I cannot see it? What has God done with me in the past which illustrates the point here? How can I encourage myself from that experience and from my knowledge of God and His ways?

Exodus 2: 11–23

God's strange way of preparing a person for service!

Preparation for a life of faithful service to God is often long, painful and arduous. This was the lesson that Moses had to learn before he could ever lead the people of Israel.

The next years of Moses' life are passed over in silence. However, from what we subsequently learn, it is clear that two very important things must have taken place during these 'lost' years. First, nursed by a believing mother, he must have been taught the promises of God and come to perceive, as Jochebed must have done, that he was being equipped to be the deliverer of God's people. Second, trained as a prince in the royal palace, he must have received teaching and experience which would enable him to lead the large number of Israelites.

Eventually, perhaps impatient for the glorious task which he envisaged for himself, Moses went out to visit his 'own people' (v.11). Apparently, he was over-anxious to prove himself to them for, seeing a dispute between an Egyptian and a Hebrew (or Israelite) he murdered the Egyptian. No motive is given for this act of killing. Moses, it seems, was only concerned to 'prove himself' to his own people.

But the right of leadership is not one that can be assumed: it must be earned. This is a lesson which Moses had not yet learnt. The following day he went out again to visit his people and this time saw two Israelites squabbling. Perhaps somewhat arrogantly, Moses intervened (v.13). The response he received not only indicated that the murder he had committed was known, but also that the people were not ready for his leadership. In fear of his life and with his dream shattered, Moses had then to flee the country (v.15).

The sequel is both romantic and tragically pathetic. His act of heroism in helping the daughters of the priest of Midian led to him finding a home and a wife (vv.16–21). At the same time, however, his sadness is apparent when Moses names his first son Gershom. Wistfully he reflects that 'I have become an alien in a strange land' (this is the meaning of the name 'Gershom'). For Moses, a man whose friends had been courtiers and who might have expected to marry an Egyptian princess, was married to a simple shepherdess who shared none of his culture, tastes, memories or dreams. During the long years that followed Moses must have often felt that all his training and leading by God had been a complete waste of time.

And yet things were happening, perhaps only dimly understood by Moses then. First, the name Gershom also indicated that Moses had renounced Egypt. In the future he would not look to the skills and the training of Egypt, valuable though they proved to be, but to the Lord alone. Second, Moses was also learning the most vital lesson of all for good leaders. He was suffering in such a way as would enable him best to serve those suffering Israelites whom he was called to lead. It has been well said that part of the price God Himself would one day have to pay in order to reconcile the world to Himself was the suffering of the Son of God. He had to become poor that we might be rich. And what was true both for Moses and Jesus is true for all who would walk in their footsteps.

From God's point of view, these apparently wasted years were a further necessary and final step in the equipping of Moses to be the leader of God's people.

Questions

1. *Preparation for leadership and service for God is seldom achieved quickly. What hopes do I have of future ministry and preparation for it? Am I impatient sometimes with God's training programme? What can I learn from this passage of Scripture?*

2. *God's training programme often includes difficulty, learning from our mistakes, and the need to discover through these experiences our strengths and weaknesses. As I reflect upon God's dealings with me what have I learnt about myself? What direction does God's equipping seem to be leading me in?*

Exodus 2:23–25

The God of history and our histories

God is often more ready to answer our prayers than we are prepared to take our needs to Him.

The Pharaoh who tried to kill Moses after he had murdered the Egyptian was probably Thutmosis III. When Thutmosis died many years later, the accession of Amenhotep II may have aroused hopes in the Israelites for an improvement in their situation. These hopes seem to have been quickly dashed and, at long last and with all hope now gone, the Israelites turned to the Lord for help. Typically the God of the Bible was more ready to hear them than they had been to ask and God's sympathy was such that He had already been preparing their deliverer Moses for his task!

How slow we so often are to learn the same lessons. The fact that we sometimes speak of marvellous answers to prayers for our little personal affairs indicates how little we seek and expect God to act in big ways to influence history. Yet both for Israel and ourselves this is sheer foolishness, for the history of Israel is: God promises, God remembers, God ac⁺s in salvation. What was true for Israel is no less true for us!

Questions

1. Think of events we have seen on TV or read about in the papers. What challenge and comfort might we gain from this passage as members of God's new covenant people?

2. The Bible teaches that God acts in history. How often do I think about the world around me and see if I can recognise God at work? Do I read the stories of Christians from the past and encourage myself by their experiences? Do I carefully watch my own life so as to see that God has been actively involved with me?

3. The Bible teaches that God is in control of everything in this world. Do I really believe this? Do I live and act as if it were true? What are those things that cause me to doubt God's control? What answer does this passage give to such doubts?

Exodus 3:1–10

The people God uses

After many years in the desert of Midian, Moses is ready for the great task God has planned for him. The Lord calls Moses in His own time not the time Moses himself would have chosen.

In chapter 2 we saw that God had aroused His people to seek His help to remove their slavery. Meanwhile God had been at work preparing Moses for the task of deliverer. But the time had now come for God to be *seen* to act and fulfil His promises.

The story in chapter 3 begins with the description of Moses carrying out his usual work as a shepherd. One day, while he was tending the flocks of his father-in-law (see 'Names in the Bible'), God appeared to him and commissioned him to be the leader who was to deliver the children of Israel.

It was probably the early summer when this happened. The heat in the desert would have been considerable. Because of this Moses would have been used to seeing the dry thorn bushes in the desert set alight by the sun. However, on this occasion, his attention was alerted by the fact that though the fire continued to burn, the bush was not consumed. We can well imagine his surprise and, since we are all inquisitive by nature, we can understand his desire to investigate this strange event more closely: we would have done the same!

Having gained Moses' attention in this way, the Angel of the Lord revealed Himself (vv.2,4). The Angel appears regularly in the Old Testament. Often, as here, the phrase is used of an appearance of God in a visible way. Some Christians have concluded from this that the Angel was the second person of the Trinity: the Son of God. This is possible. Certainly, the Angel is, at the same time, both described as God and yet distinguished from Him. The very least that can be said is that this Angel prepares the reader of the Bible for the fuller revelation of God as three-in-one in the New Testament.

Normally, in the Bible, fire is a symbol of God's holiness; so it is in this story. In many parts of the world people are expected to remove their shoes or sandals when entering a place of worship. This act represents the removal of uncleanness caused by contact with the world. It is a recognition of the holiness of God. All this explains God's request to Moses in verse 5.

Wonderfully, though, the holy God appeared to Moses the sinner as a friend. We are not told at this point in the story how this could be so. However, the later chapters of Exodus devote many chapters to explaining this marvellous mystery.

The Angel of the Lord quickly explained why He had appeared to Moses. The Lord was the same God who had made the promises to Abraham, Isaac and Jacob (v.6). Those promises were now to be fulfilled (vv.8,9). In response to the people's prayer for help (v.7) God was going to save His people at last!

The God of the Bible uses men and women to achieve His purposes. He has no need to do so. However, he humbly invites us to share with Him in the fulfilling of His plans. What a remarkable privilege! In this story this privilege is given to Moses. God was going to save His people but Moses was the person chosen by God to achieve it.

Questions

1. *On what basis do we choose leaders in our churches? Are the things we look for the same as those that the Lord is especially concerned to find in His servants?*

2. *The Bible insists that God is a holy God. Thinking about this passage do I show that I really believe this by the way that I live and by the way I worship Him?*

3. *God uses men and women to achieve His purposes and to answer prayer. Could God be calling us to answer some of the prayers that we are making? Do we really believe that God could use someone like ourselves to bring Him glory?*

Names in the Bible

Some people are puzzled by the fact that Moses' father-in-law is given at least two different names in the Bible. But should we be surprised when this happens here (and on other occasions in the Bible)? Most of us have several names: our first names and surnames, nicknames and pet names. We are known by different names on different occasions or situations. Thus, Moses' father-in-law is here given what was probably his 'public' name: Jethro. In 2:18 he was called Reuel which was probably his 'family' name.

Exodus 3:11–22

The call of God

Moses argues with God that he is not equipped for the task to which he is being called. God's reply to Moses (and to us) is that God's calling is enough to make sure that he has everything he needs.

Years earlier Moses would have quickly welcomed the invitation God was now making to him. Indeed he had once tried to become the champion of the children of Israel (2:11–14). However, the years of bitterness and hardship in the land of Midian had changed him. In place of the bold, impetuous and impatient man of previous years was the timid, hesitant and diffident Moses of the present story. During the years in the desert he had learned of his own weaknesses and limitations. And yet his former hopes do not seem to have completely vanished. The questions he asked God when invited to lead the people were, mostly, sensible ones. They suggested that over the years he had thoughtfully considered what his needs would be if God ever called him to the task which he had once tried to undertake alone.

There is a lesson here for all Christians. God sometimes calls us to do things that seem utterly impossible. The impossibility itself should not discourage us (as it so often does). However, we are not expected to be reckless. Like Moses we are to give careful thought to the resources we need and then seek them from God. There would be far fewer casualties among Christian workers if they had all followed the example of Moses.

Moses' first question is made and answered in verses 11–13. He argued that he was not adequate to undertake God's task for him. In answer to this, God tells him: 'I will be with you'. Where Moses' abilities might fail there was to be a God with unlimited abilities. This must have been as great a comfort to Moses as it ought to be to us. When we are at the end of our resources we are not at the end of His: nor can we ever be!

It is natural for anyone who is asked to do something adventurous to seek guarantees that there will be success. Often Christians who are called to do a great work for God are also tempted to seek a sign from God. The story of Gideon and his fleece (Judges 6:36–40) is often used to encourage such sign-seeking. However, the Bible forbids the seeking of a sign or the putting of God to the test (Exod 17:2; Deut 6:16, etc.). This suggests that perhaps Gideon was wrong to seek a sign and his request showed his lack of faith. Even so, God was merciful to him, as He often is to us, and met Gideon's request twice! There is, however, no excuse for our faithlessness. God tested the faith of Gideon to the limit later.

Moses did not, however, seek a sign although God did offer him one. But what a strange sign it was! God told Moses that his success in delivering the people would prove the Lord was with him. In fact this is the truest sign of all. The Lord says to us all: 'Go, and your success will show that I am with you'. Reinforced by the assurance of God's presence we should need no further guarantee to our faith.

Moses' second question is recorded in verse 13. The reason for his question is, however, not immediately clear. There is a widespread superstition in many parts of the world that the knowledge of a person's name is able to give special power to anyone who knows it. It is possible that this sort of idea lay behind Moses' request. However, it is more likely that Moses' words reflect a belief that a new revelation of God would be accompanied by a new name. Perhaps Moses also wished to know what to say about God to the people of Israel. This is likely because in Old Testament times the name of a person often reflected a person's character. Moses was probably asking God: 'What fresh insight into your character are you going to show me which will strengthen your people in the days ahead?'

It is one of the most frequent weaknesses of God's people that they do not build their faith on that which God has revealed about Himself. The inevitable result of this failure is seen in the spiritual instability of so many believers. To build on any other foundation than God and His promises is bound to lead to this sad result. For good reason, then, Moses sought a fresh revelation of God appropriate to his own needs and those of God's people.

Questions

1. *God sometimes weighs down His people with a vision for His work that seems impossible to fulfil. Have we such a burden and, if so, what might we learn from this passage as to how to check whether this is God's call for us? And what might we do in order to see God's purposes realised?*

2. *We are to build our faith on what God has revealed about Himself. Do I do this? What does God tell me about Himself in this passage which I ought to build on?*

Exodus 3:11–22 (continued)

The ever present God

Moses is promised that he will enter into a battlefield if he faithfully undertakes the Lord's wishes. But he is also promised, as we are, the presence of God with him in all that he seeks to do for the Lord.

God's reply to Moses seeking fresh knowledge of God is recorded in verses 14 and 15. God repeats His name, known and used by His people for many years before, but explains its meaning. His name is Yahweh he reminds Moses, and this means 'I am'.

Christians have, for a long time, discussed the exact meaning of God's reply. Some have concluded that the answer is no real answer at all! They suggest that God said: 'I will be the person I prove to be'. However, it is more likely that a clear answer to Moses' question *was* given and that verse 15 is intended to provide it. God's reply to Moses was intended to emphasise that He will be the ever present and faithful God: just as He had been with Abraham, Isaac and Jacob when He had made such great promises to them. One of the New Testament writers makes the same point about Jesus who 'is the same yesterday, today and forever' (Heb 13:8).

Assured now of God's presence Moses was commanded by the Lord to go to the children of Israel. He was to tell them 'God has promised; God has heard; God will deliver' (vv.16–17). He was also assured that his message would be well received (v.18). The life of many believers and churches would be transformed if they, too, built their faith on God and His promises. Yet we so often fail although we can have as great a knowledge of God as Moses had.

To the reader who lives in western society the next part of the story often creates difficulties. Moses was commanded to go to Pharaoh and demand, not freedom, but a three day journey into the desert for a religious festival. This, it is suggested, was dishonest of Moses because he was really seeking nothing less than complete freedom.

However, readers who live in other parts of the world will see little difficulty here. They will be familiar with the complicated bargaining procedures in their own societies and will recognise Moses' demand for complete freedom in his words. Moses was speaking politely. However, he was asking to go three days' journey beyond the Egyptian frontier. Pharaoh would have known from the start that this implied that the people would never return. After all, they were only tolerated immigrants. Pharaoh would have no claim on them once they had left his land.

Pharaoh was, of course, the most powerful man in the ancient world. He was also recognised as a god. It would have been quite natural for him to assume that the god of a slave people was inferior to him and the gods of Egypt. Only after clear proof that this was not so would he submit to the demands of the slave people's god. The Lord knew this and warned Moses (vv.19,20). Moses was about to enter a battlefield. And yet the victory was assured. Pharaoh would be forced to submit to the Lord's demands and the Egyptians would willingly hand over their treasures to the followers of such a powerful god (vv.21,22).

The victory for Moses was certain. But the path to it would be far from easy. This is something we need to learn. The New Testament reminds us many, many times that disciples of the Lord Jesus are on the victorious side. Equally often, those same Scriptures remind us that victory is rarely achieved except through long, difficult and painful battles (e.g. Acts 14:22). Sin and the Devil, our greatest enemies, do not willingly give up their power – like Pharaoh. Just as Moses had to rely by faith on the promises in dark days of apparent defeat, so do we.

Questions

1. *God is always present with His people. Do we really believe this? If we do, what difference should it make to the situations we are faced with at the moment?*

2. *God seldom achieves His purposes without His people experiencing many tests to their faith. What can I learn from this passage which will help me prepare for my service of God or which can help me in my present difficulties?*

Exodus 4:1–17

A ministry of wonders and weakness

Moses receives the guarantees which confirm his calling, but he learns, too, that all service of God is undertaken in personal weakness. God does not change and the lessons of this passage are no less relevant today.

Moses could be criticised for his third question to God (v.1). God had already promised that the children of Israel would listen to him (3:18). Surely that promise should have been enough for Moses? However, he was aware of the fact that God's people might not be persuaded by the promised sign of worshipping on God's mountain. They would need something more to make them believe God's messenger. In the New Testament we read of 'the signs of an apostle' (2 Cor 12:12) and in the Old Testament God often confirmed the authority of His messengers by miraculous signs. Elijah and Elisha are two good examples of this. Moses' question in verse 1 need not, therefore, be seen as evidence of unbelief. Probably he was simply asking God: 'Where are the signs which will confirm my ministry to the children of Israel?'.

In response God gave Moses three signs: the rod which turned into a snake (vv.2–5); the leprous hand (vv.6,7) and the changing of the water of the Nile into blood (vv.8,9). These signs were given to confirm Moses' authority and promote belief in his message (see, especially, vv.5,8).

Sometimes today God confirms His message with miraculous signs.

However, it is more important for us to notice the way in which God confirmed Jesus' ministry. Jesus was the Word of God in a unique way (John 1:1–18). He showed God's way to men and women more fully than anyone else could do. He did many miracles and spoke as no-one else ever did (Matt 7:28–9; 8:27). Above all, however, He rose from the dead: a fact confirmed by many reliable witnesses (Acts 1:3). There can be no greater sign than that! This should lead us to faith in Him: there is no lack of evidence that Jesus is God's Word.

In many societies it is the eloquent man or woman who is listened to and respected. The ancient world was no different. Moses' fourth question is, therefore, understandable. He doubted his own ability to speak in such a way as to command a hearing. There is nothing to suggest that Moses' assessment was incorrect. However, at this stage in his conversation with the Lord his faith ought to have been strong enough to overcome such doubts. God's assurance that He would help him speak was not enough (v.11). Moses still hesitated (v.13). His natural humility had become stubbornness and this provoked the Lord to anger (v.14). And yet, in mercy, God met Moses half way: Aaron, his brother and an eloquent speaker, was appointed as Moses' spokesman.

Earlier, we noticed that when God calls us to a work we should not be reckless. Equally true is the lesson contained in these verses. All too easily humility can lead to a refusal of God's call. In the end, however, it is not our sense of weakness but the Lord's call which is to be the deciding factor in our obedience.

Questions

1. People around us sometimes ask for facts to back up the truth of the Christian message. What lessons might we learn from this passage to answer such a request?

2. Jesus rose, as He predicted, from the dead. This miracle stands at the centre of the Christian faith. Do we build our faith on this great foundation? There may sometimes be other signs but this sign guarantees our forgiveness, the removal of our guilt and assures our future destiny. By faith, do we believe this?

3. It is God's way to work through weak, feeble people to achieve His plans. Do I use my weaknesses as an excuse for not doing what I ought to do for Him? Am I conscious of His call upon my life but hiding behind my sense of feebleness? What can I learn from this passage to guide, help and challenge me?

Exodus 4:1–17 (continued)

The Word of God and the servant of the Lord

God spoke through Moses, as He did with all His special servants, so that Moses actually spoke God's very words! What importance we ought to give to the recorded words of the Lord's special servants.

Before we leave these verses, there are two other important matters which require our attention.

In verses 15 and 16 the Lord told Moses to be like God to Aaron. He then explained what He meant. Just as God put *words* in the mouths of His messengers, so Moses is to do the same with Aaron. This is how God speaks His word to us. When we read the words of God's messengers in the Bible we read God's Word.

This is very important. Many people think that Bible reading is like mining. A miner looks among valueless rocks for precious stones or metal. So it is suggested that we are to look among the words of men for the words of God. These verses tell us that this is a wrong idea. Without explaining how God achieved it, these verses teach us that all the words of God's servants in the Bible are God's words. We simply cannot pick and choose among them.

We need also to notice that chapters 3:1–4:17 teach us that God planned to deliver His people through one man or mediator. We are told five things about Moses:

1. He was an ordinary man;
2. Yet he spoke God's words and revealed God to men and women;
3. He brought the presence of God to the children of Israel – (3:12: 'I will be with you');
4. He was appointed by God to do two things: to break the power of Pharaoh (3:20) and to plunder Egypt (3:21–22);
5. Finally, he was a sinner (compare 3:5,6 with Gen 3:8,10).

This last point is very important. God had promised Adam that one day a person would come to defeat sin once and for all time. God promised Abraham that it was from his descendants that this great leader would come. He also promised Abraham a land in which his descendants would live. That land would be like Eden. Could Moses, then, be the great deliverer? The answer is: 'No'. Moses, a sinner, could not conquer sin!

However, the Old Testament writers did recognise that what Moses did was a shadowy picture of what God would one day do through someone else. The New Testament tell us that this 'someone' was Jesus. With this in mind we need to note three things about Jesus:

1. Jesus was both God and man. He was the great revealer of God (John 1:1,14,18). We are to listen, above all, to Him (Matt 17:5).
2. Jesus was without sin (Heb 4:15). However, as a man He was able to sympathise with sinners (Heb 4:15; 5:2) and yet also make the perfect offering for sin (Heb 10:4,10; 9:15).
3. In this way Jesus was able to plunder not Pharaoh but the power of Satan in order that we might live to God (Eph 1:20–21; Rom 7:1–4).

Questions

1. *Where should we guide non Christians if they want to meet with God and hear Him speak to them?*
2. *The Bible is the words of God to us. If we believe this, do we act as though it is true? How should we see Bible study and listening to those God has called to teach His words?*
3. *Jesus was God and man united in one person but without sin. What can I learn from this passage about Him and what He came to do for me?*

Exodus 4:18–28

Trusting a sovereign God

Moses discovered that obeying God brought with it a sense of assurance that God was with him. This is an important lesson which we all need to learn.

These verses are rather like a bridge. They describe Moses' final preparations in Midian and his return to Egypt, where the next part of the story is to take place.

Moses (and Aaron) had been called to follow and serve the Lord just as we are called to be disciples of the Lord Jesus. However, before they could serve God fully there were some important lessons to be learned: lessons equally relevant to all of us.

Verses 18–23 briefly record the account of Moses tidying up his affairs in Midian and packing for the return journey to Egypt. In so doing, they record his immediate obedience to the call of God.

It is possible that the words of God recorded in verses 19,21–23 followed immediately on the Lord's conversation with Moses in verse 17. However, it is more probable that these words were given to Moses at the precise point at which they are recorded in the story. If this is so, they teach some very important truths. Moses had been called by God to serve Him. After some hesitation he obeyed. And obedience brought with it God's confirmation. The Lord dealt with the natural anxieties of Moses concerning those who had sought his life and re-affirmed Moses' calling.

The Lord often deals with us in the same way. Moses' obedience was not to depend on confirmatory signs; he must trust God. But God did give a number of signs to encourage Moses' obedience to His will. We suggested above that success is its own confirmation of our calling of God to some task. But this is, in fact, not the full story. Success would eventually follow from Moses' ministry. In the meanwhile, God graciously gave Moses an ever increasing assurance that He was with him.

Far too many Christians are awaiting special confirmation of God's will when the Lord has made His will quite plain to them. Similarly, too many have such a shallow faith that it must be supported by 'signs' before they can be aroused to obedience. Finally, there are many who equate the Lord's will with success and happiness. This part of Moses' life rebukes all of these false assumptions.

The phrase 'But I will harden Pharaoh's heart' has given Christians down the years great difficulty. The difficulty is more imagined than real. The Bible teaches the sovereignty of God in all things. He made everything from nothing (Heb 11:3) even the spirit world (Ps 148:2,5). He also controls everything all the time. God is the author of all new discoveries. Farming, technological and even military skills come from Him (Isa 28:26; 54:16; Ps 144:1). He controls everything: season by season, day by day and moment by moment (Acts 14:17; Isa 40:26; Matt 6:30). Even the most insignificant things are under God's constant control (Matt 10:30). The Bible states that the destinies of individual men and women are in His hands (Eph 1:11) and that not only are disasters under His control (Amos 3:6) but God can use evil for His own ends (Acts 2:23). However, alongside this the Bible insists that human beings are responsible for their actions and their freedom to make decisions is a real one.

The Bible is content to live with both these truths and to build on them. It is happy to leave the resolution of the apparent contradiction in the hands of God and not try to explain away one truth by appeal to the other. We should follow its example: delighting in God's sovereignty and taking our own responsibility very seriously indeed. The example of Pharaoh is an illustration of all of this. Though God hardened his heart, it is stated elsewhere that Pharaoh hardened his own heart, or, his heart was hard (Ex 7:13; 8:15). This preserves the balance of the Bible.

These verses also mention for the first time that Israel was the 'first-born' of God. They were His chosen people; His favourites. Thus, because Pharaoh would not release God's first-born, he suffered the loss of his own.

Questions

1. *God is sovereign ruler over all things but His people are fully responsible for their lives before Him. Do we really believe this? What challenge or comfort might these twin beliefs bring to our present situation and needs?*

2. *God's call to His children is often very clear. To check up on it is an act of unbelief. Are there areas in my own life where I know God's will but refuse to obey, perhaps hiding behind a spiritual-sounding excuse?*

Exodus 4:18–28 (continued)

The way of obedience

God expects all His children to faithfully obey Him. It is also characteristic of Him to discipline those of us who err.

Verses 24–26 are among the strangest in the whole of the Bible. Yet, although the details are not easy to understand, the point of the story is very clear. God had commanded Abraham and his descendants to circumcise their male children (Gen 17:10). It was the sign that they were the Lord's. However, Moses seems to have dis-obeyed this command and one of his sons was uncircumcised. Probably this was under pressure from Zipporah his wife. Such disobedience was such as to place a person outside of God's people. The reason for this was that circumcision was the proper response to God's grace. It symbolised the response of the heart (Jer 9:26; Rom 2:29). Thus, if God must punish disobedient Pharaoh, He must also punish Moses.

In this way God taught Moses that no-one has a right to claim the privileges of God's people unless he or she is obedient to God's commands. In the New Testament many Christians feel that baptism occupies a similar place to circumcision in the Old Testament. The proper response to God's display of love in Jesus is faith and baptism. In the New Testament baptism is the response of faith. Faith without baptism is defective and disobedient Christianity. An unbaptised believer has only made a partial response to the gospel. In the fullest sense such a person is not truly Christian. Moses had to learn to obey fully in a very dramatic way!

We meet Aaron for the first time in verses 27–28. Because of the later incident with the golden calf (chapters 32–34) he has often been regarded badly by Christians. However, fewer of his failings are recorded in the Bible than those of Moses himself. Certainly, we need to notice that, when God spoke to him, he was immediately obedient. This was so even though Moses was his younger brother and Aaron may have already been an important leader among the people of Israel. (The title 'Levite' given to Aaron may well suggest he had some public authority. Compare also 4:14 and 7:7.) Nevertheless Aaron was willing to be Moses' spokesman.

When God speaks to us we are not to be too proud to be servants. We are to be willing to do whatever He asks us to do and to regard it as a privilege. Sadly, despite the example of Jesus (Matt 20:26–28 and Phil 2:5–11) we so often fail in this.

Questions

1. *If this passage teaches us that God must discipline even His own children what might we suppose it teaches about His attitude to non Christians? What consequences ought this to have for us?*

2. *Obedience through thick and thin is the only sure sign of a child of God. Do we presume upon God's favour while failing to obey Him in every area of our lives? Are there areas of our life and work where we try to keep God at a distance and do what we want to do?*

3. *True ministry for God is always a ministry of service to others. What attitude do I have towards my own service for God? Am I willing to become like a slave and do the least honourable tasks for Him? If I have a responsibility in the local church do I cling to the honour it brings or see it as a ground for my serving others still more fully?*

Exodus 4:29–5:21

A ministry begun and which ends in failure

Faithfulness to God does not always bring instant success and popularity. Moses and Aaron found their initial steps in obedience surrounded by hardship and failure.

These verses describe the beginning of Moses and Aaron's ministry...and its complete failure. By chapter 5:21 the situation in Egypt is worse than when they had arrived!

Yet things had begun so well. The people of Israel had responded as they should have done to Moses and Aaron's news (4:29–31). Despite their great difficulties and needs they rejoiced and gave thanks to God. Many Christian leaders have been appointed to lead God's people amid such high hopes and confidence in God. However, the situation soon changed for Moses. Often the same is true today.

Strengthened by the people's response the two brothers went to Pharaoh. Immediately, they made a mistake. In chapter 4:18 Moses had been given the words with which to address Pharaoh. But the words which Aaron says to the king are quite different. In place of a polite request is a firm command (v.1). Pharaoh's response was therefore predictable, for none of us likes being told what to do. And Pharaoh would have thought: 'Who is this god who dares make such demands of me, the god-king of Egypt?' Moses and Aaron quickly realised their mistake and made their second request in far more polite terms (v.3).

But the damage had been done. Just like so many before and since, Pharaoh responded by meeting what he saw as unrest with increased repression. This is fully described in the following verses (6–19), as is its result. The early support given to Moses by the people was soon followed by rejection and blame being heaped on the brothers. The Israelite leaders both ignored Moses and Aaron (vv.15–17) and then blamed them (vv.18–21).

There is something very familiar to us about all of this. The glory of God is often achieved only through suffering and hardship. Frequently, difficulties come right at the beginning when the impetus of a work has not been established. A work stopped before it has begun is a great victory for Satan. However, it is not this precise point which is being taught here. Rather, the passage teaches us that it is *God's purpose* to surround the path of His people with difficulty (4:21)! He often sets His final glory against the background of dark despair and opposition on every side. He does this to display His glory more fully. Just as Moses was driven to the Lord by such an experience, so God often intends to make us come in total dependence to Him and to look nowhere else.

Sadly, the response of God's people to Moses and Aaron is also paralleled in many Christian leaders' experience. The Lord Jesus had a similar thing happen to Him (see Mark 11:9–10 and 15:13). We are also expected to remember His words: 'A student is not above his teacher, nor a servant above his master' (Matt 10:24). What happened to Jesus will often happen to us! What the people had to learn was that the promises of God and the call to Moses had not changed. The people had to realise that to expect blessing without trial is seldom God's purpose. In their rejection of Moses they showed the poverty of their own faith (v.21).

Some believers collapse under difficulty. Others see the difficulties as opportunities for God to manifest His glory. This passage shows that the latter are right!

Questions

1. *If God's purposes are not always accompanied by instant success, how should non Christians view the apparent failure of the Christian church today?*

2. *God often accomplishes His purposes through our own hardship and suffering. What expectations do we have for our ministry for God? What lessons and encouragement can we draw from this passage during times of difficulty?*

3. *God's leaders often experience discouragement at the hands of God's people. Can I trace God's purposes through times of darkness? Do I have sufficient confidence in Him when the way gets tough? In what way may I sometimes discourage those who are seeking to lead in my church?*

Exodus 5:22–7:7

Arguing with God and standing on His promises

Troubled Moses discovers that God is ready to hear his doubts and answer his questions with words of reassurance. The same remains true for us too!

In their trials the people of God tried to help themselves and failed (5:15–19). Moses, however, turned to the Lord (5:22–23). He looked to the only One who could help. How often at the point of our deepest need we forget that God alone can give us security and hope.

Moses was willing to argue with God. He pointed out that the situation had turned out just as he, Moses, had said it would. When believers in the Bible were in difficulties, they often argued with God. Unfortunately, when we are afflicted we are usually unwilling to open our hearts to God. Perhaps we think that complaining to the Lord is sin. But surely it is a greater sin not to turn to Him at all! Moreover, it is not wrong to ask: 'Why?'. It is the privilege of children to discuss things with their parents. The same is true of us and our heavenly father.

Moses quickly discovered that God was not only willing to hear his questions, but was also ready to meet him in his needs. Moses discovered that when help was needed the Lord was never absent. The same is true for each one of us.

When God answered Moses, he reminded him of a number of great facts. Moses was reminded that God was far more powerful than Pharaoh.

Although Moses had been discouraged by the power of the king, God's own 'mighty hand' would force reluctant Pharaoh to *expel* the Israelites. It is very easy for believers to over-estimate the power of the hostile sinful world and even the Devil himself. Too many of us think of the power of God and His enemies as almost equal. While the Bible is well aware of the power of sin and the evil one, it never teaches that they are equal with the power of God. God's enemies may be powerful but His strength is much, much greater than theirs! So Moses was reminded that it was the Lord not Pharaoh whose hand was 'mighty'. And, just in case Moses was not listening carefully, the claim was made twice!

Perhaps this reminder should have been enough for Moses. But God is not miserly in the help He gives His children. Moses was reminded of two other facts. First, he was told once again of the promises of God (vv.2–5). These promises would have now been very familiar to Moses. God had spoken to Abraham, Isaac and Jacob (see Gen 12:1-3; 17:7,8, etc.) and these words had been recited to Moses from childhood. God Himself had repeated them to Moses (4:7–10). Now He said them once more. God's promises had not changed even though Moses was experiencing difficulties. As Christians we rarely build our faith on the promises of God in times of trouble. As a result, we lose the comfort and strength that those promises are able to bring to us.

Questions

1. *The Bible story is one which is based around certainties: God promises and is powerful enough to do what He says. Do we build our faith around those things that God has promised us in the Bible and are we sure that He cannot fail? What promises in the Bible and what truths about God do we need to apply to our situation today?*

2. *Christians have a heavenly father. What is the ideal picture I have of an earthly father? Do I believe that those things which I have in my picture (friendship and care, love and an ability to keep on loving despite all my weaknesses) are true of God too? How might such beliefs change and deepen my attitude and relationship to God?*

Exodus 5:22–7:7 (continued)

Fellowship with God is followed by failure in service

Moses discovers the necessary truth that despite the evidence of God's care it is so easy for faith to fail almost immediately.

God had not finished with teaching Moses. Lastly, Moses was reminded of the tender love of God (v.5). A mother's care for her child may cease but God's love never ends. That love guarantees that God will stand by His children. This is what the Lord sought to teach Moses. In the New Testament the same truth is taught.

The writer to the Hebrews reminded his readers that the Lord Jesus was a man subject to weakness (but not sin). As a result of this He was and is able to sympathise with those whom He loves. Yet the same Lord Jesus now lives in heaven where all power is His. The conclusion is as wonderful as it is inevitable: 'Let us then approach the throne of grace with confidence, so that we may receive mercy and find grace to help us in our time of need' (Heb 4:16).

Having reminded Moses of these great truths about Himself, the Lord proceeded to assure Moses (6:6–8). These verses include seven assurances which are 'bracketed' by the double reminder: 'I am the Lord'. Thus:

I am the Lord
I will bring you out;
I will redeem you;

I will take you as my own people;
I will be your God;
I will bring you to the land;
I will give it to you as a possession,
I am the Lord.

In this way God guaranteed to fulfil all His promises: a fact which was the more certain because His character as the 'Lord' demanded it (see 'God's Name').

Sadly, however, when Moses went to speak to the people again they were not interested in hearing from either him or his God (v.9). It is, therefore, not surprising that when God asked him once again to go and speak to Pharaoh that Moses raised old excuses (vv.10–12). The Bible is refreshingly honest when it describes its heroes. Very often we tend to distort the truth and cover over the weaknesses of great men and women. But the Bible tells us about such people with all their weaknesses. There is good reason for this. We can immediately identify our own experiences with people like Moses and we can learn from them. We cannot learn from 'supermen or women'.

And how like Moses we are. He was refreshed by the Lord. Yet Moses' memory was so short that at the first obstacle he fell once more. But God was not finished with him. What mercy our God showed to him and still shows to us!

At this point the story is interrupted by a list of Moses' ancestors (vv.13–27). While in certain parts of the world the information recorded here may be of great interest (it tells us who Moses was), yet for others it rather frustratingly breaks into the story. However, in so doing, it heightens the tension: 'What will happen next?' we eagerly ask. Perhaps both these reactions were intended by the author of Exodus, who was probably Moses himself (see 'Who wrote Exodus?').

Before we leave the list there is one thing we ought to add. The Bible is full of similar lists and we are tempted to ignore them when reading the Scriptures. However, the very fact that God has preserved these lists is a testimony to how interested He is in individuals. So often we can feel a very insignificant part of a nation or people. The Creator of the world, however, is deeply interested in individuals – ordinary people just like ourselves.

In 6:9–12 we left the story of Moses at the point where further discouragement had brought him back to the Lord, once again to plead his weakness. The intervening verses have only served to increase the interest in the question of what God will do following this further failure by Moses. The Lord's response is a great encouragement for those of us who, like

55

Moses, fail so often. Moses was not rebuked. Once again God met him in his need. Moses was reminded again that the path to glory is through difficulty (compare 4:28–5:21) but that victory is assured. For those of us who are inclined to think that this point is made rather frequently in Exodus, it is important to remember how short our memories so often are in spiritual matters. If Moses needed reminding we may be sure the same is true of us! So we may learn that we can never come too often to the Lord and plead 'I believe, help my unbelief'.

Questions

1. *God is deeply interested in ordinary people. Do we sometimes consider ourselves to be too insignificant to be of any use to God or of interest to Him? Are there ways in which we can take the truths in this section of Scripture so as to help us to discover His love and mercy for us?*

2. *God is so faithful to His frail, erring people. Do I feel very weak as a believer? Do I carry a burden of failure in God's service? What lessons can I learn in this passage which assure me of God's forgiveness and continuing love for me?*

God's Name

In most Bible versions God is sometimes referred to as 'LORD' (in capital letters). At other times it is printed 'Lord'. The reason for this difference in printing the name of God is that in the Old Testament two different words are used. Translators render 'Yahweh' as LORD and 'adonai' as 'Lord'.

Adonai is also used, in a more general way, of 'lords and masters'. When used of God it emphasises His mastery of the world and the calling of men and women to live as His servants.

Yahweh is quite different. It is like a christian or forename of God, rather as mine is Stephen. It is like a name which the family and close friends use. As such it is a lovely reminder of the relationship Christians have with God. We are His slaves, friends, and even more wonderfully, sons and daughters!

Exodus 6:3 has raised much discussion because though the Lord says: 'By my name "the LORD" I did not make myself known to...Abraham, Isaac and Jacob', 'the LORD' is mentioned in Genesis. There are several possible explanations. The author of Genesis may have used the later name when telling an earlier story. It is also possible that though the name was known, its implications were not. This seems the most likely explanation.

Who wrote Exodus?

For many centuries it was assumed that Moses was the author of the first five books of the Bible (probably excluding the account of his death in Deuteronomy 34 and one or two other passages which might have been added later).

This view became increasingly challenged in the eighteenth and nineteenth centuries. It was suggested, for example, that writing had not been invented at the time that Moses was alleged to have lived. It was also argued that the first five books show evidence of being an anthology of other books and that the first edition of the Pentateuch (Genesis to Deuteronomy) was not completed until the sixth century BC. Anyone suggesting Moses wrote Exodus was laughed at (and still is in certain places!).

However, we now know that writing was invented well before the time of Moses and it is increasingly recognised that the theory of editing for the Pentateuch is a practical impossibility.

There is no reason to believe that Moses could not have written Exodus and the other books and certainly much of the material claims to have come from him. His unique upbringing in Pharaoh's household would have also provided him with the necessary skills to undertake the work.

Increasingly, it appears likely that Moses was the author of most, if not all, of the Pentateuch.

Exodus 7:8–11:10

The revelation of God and the response of men

In these chapters God seeks to awaken and strengthen faith in Himself. At the same time the character and folly of unbelief is plainly set out. We are intended to learn the lesson well!

People who have some knowledge of the Bible usually know the stories in the next five chapters of Exodus. The plagues are among the first stories taught to young children because they are so able to grip the imagination. However, these true tales were not intended to be only good stories. They also contain the message of God: a
message as important today as it was when the events actually took place.

Two different words are used to describe the plagues. They were 'blows' and 'signs'. They were intended to be both judgments and signs which taught the reality and character of the Lord. In this way we can see that they were not vindictive actions by God but acts of mercy intended to arouse repentance and faithful obedience.

One of the Biblical answers to the problem of suffering and evil lies here. By His 'blows' God tries to arouse us to seek Him. In these chapters the faith of the Israelites was rekindled (compare 5:21; 6:9 with 10:1–2). The Lord responds to Pharaoh's challenge (5:2) by a display of His incomparable power (9:14). Sadly, though, the king refused to submit to Him. Sometimes Christians foolishly think that all that is required to persuade others to become Christians is a mighty display of the power of God.

However, the signs are not enough. Men and women may know the truth but still refuse the Lord. Pharaoh is a vivid example of this. Jesus was right when He said: 'They will not be convinced even if someone rises from the dead' (Luke 16:31). The evidence of 2,000 years of history confirms this. There is no lack of evidence to support the claims of the Christian. More important is the question of whether people are prepared to take notice and respond to that evidence.

Before we look at these chapters in detail it is helpful to set out the main lessons which they are intended to teach. The first purpose of these chapters is to emphasise that the Lord calls us all to obedient trust in Him. God requires implicit trust in His word (9:20–21). In these chapters God gradually removed all the other things that might have claimed the authority which was His alone. For example, the priest-magicians were embarrassed and conquered (8:19; 9:11); the gods of Egypt, which were the true opponents in many of the plagues (see below), were humbled before the Creator (9:14); the magicians' claims that the plagues were inexplicably 'supernatural' (8:19) – which is the meaning of the phrase 'the finger of God' – was overturned. To suggest that something is 'supernatural' avoids the real issue. But Pharaoh was finally forced beyond this excuse to acknowledge his guilt before the Creator (9:27).

How like us Pharaoh was! How often must the Lord first break us before we confess Him. Yet how loving His discipline is! He desires our loving obedience rather than let us march unrebuked to eternal damnation.

These chapters also show us that there is a response to God which falls short of that which the Lord seeks. Despite Pharaoh's confession (9:27) Moses was only too well aware that it fell short of true reverence (9:30). Moses was soon proved right (9:34; 10:16,20). The king's confession had been effected by the sheer force of the plague. His was the self-centred statement of someone who had been unwillingly cornered. What God sought, and still seeks, is willing self-renunciation and unqualified trust in Himself. Less than this will not avert God's final judgment (11:1–10). Only this plucks us from hell.

Finally, we need to notice the great danger of persistent rebellion against God. Throughout the plagues, and despite them, Pharaoh would not yield (7:13–14,23; 8:15,19,32; 9:7). Eventually, the Lord stopped dealing mercifully with him (9:15) and confirmed him in his rebellion (9:12; 10:1,20,27). Judgment (11:1-10) became inevitable.

The Lord has not changed. He continues daily to call us to Himself. He does this through the world of 'nature' (Rom 1:18–20); through His control of nations and individual lives (Acts 17:26–27) and in the hearts and consciences of men and women (Rom 2:14–15). He does it through suffering and trial. Above all, God calls through His Word in the Bible and by His messengers. At the same time He warns us to act now (Psalm 95:7–11). Sooner than we think, the time for response may have passed and despite all His invitations we may, like Pharaoh, be 'hardened' in our sins.

Questions

1. How does this passage apply to non Christians and how might we speak to our neighbours about the Lord in the light of the lessons set out here?

2. God calls us all to obedient trust in Him. In what areas of our lives is God calling us to trust Him today? Are there areas of our lives (and our church lives) in which He has been calling us to obedience? What can we learn from this passage to encourage us to trust and obey God?

3. God must punish persistent rebellion against His will. Are there plans, thoughts or actions that I have or do which displease God? How long do I think that I can go on disobeying the loving God? Do I so emphasise His love as to forget that He must and will punish all sin?

Exodus 7:8–8:19

Danger! The God of gods at work

The leaders of Egypt are forced to recognise that Moses and Aaron are no mere magicians but that they are the servants of one who has supernatural powers.

After setting his credentials before Pharaoh and his court (7:8–13) the first plague was brought upon Egypt: the plague of blood. This would have been a great inconvenience to the Egyptians since the Nile was the centre of the life of the nation and fish was the most important food of the Egyptians. Far more important than this, however, was the fact that the Nile was worshipped as a god. Thus, the plague would have been seen as a challenge by the Lord against one of the gods of ancient Egypt (see 'The Plagues and the gods of ancient Egypt'): a challenge which resulted in total victory for the Israelite God.

It is not clear what exactly happened when this plague occurred. Some have suggested that we are not intended to understand that the Nile waters changed literally into blood. It is said that what probably happened is that a considerable volume of red earth was brought down from the Abyssinian highlands from where the Nile waters came. This would have poisoned the river and killed the fish. There would have been little that was unusual in this – except, of course, the quantity of silt brought down by the river. Most of the plagues can be explained in a similar way.

What are we to make of such suggestions? Many of us tend to divide our possible experiences into two groups. On the one hand there are events that we describe as 'natural'. These are things that we can explain by our knowledge of how things usually work and function. Supernatural events (should they occur) are miracles: things that seem to have no explanation, or happen in such a way as to break the usual rules of nature.

The Bible does not think in this way. It knows that the whole world is ordered by God and so ordered that many events can be described as natural. On the other hand, it speaks of 'signs' which are events that point, in a special way, to the presence of God. To have any real meaning these signs are accompanied before, during or after by a word from God. Otherwise they are simply unexplained events. Signs may be completely miraculous. Sometimes, however, it is the unusual nature of what happens or its timing that makes it a sign. Thus some of the signs in the book of Exodus may have a natural explanation: but they are no less miraculous because of this.

However, it is characteristic of God's dealings with men and women that His signs are usually capable of a different interpretation. Coincidences can be ignored. Usually He does not force us to acknowledge Him. The sign can be ignored. There is enough evidence for belief. There is also enough to enable us to persist in unbelief if we want to. This is quite a deliberate act of God. He wants a people who will serve Him because they want to: not because they must. Thus, Pharaoh, having seen the 'miracles' of his own magicians chose to ignore God's sign (7:22–23). Do you, perhaps, hide behind such excuses and refuse to believe the good news of Jesus?

Like so many before and since Pharaoh took little notice of something which only inconvenienced others! However, the second plague, the Frogs (8:1–15) affected him (v.3) and forced him to arrange an audience with Moses and Aaron. He gave two reasons. The first; 'Pray to the Lord to take the frogs away *from me* and my people' (v.8). The second was a promise of freedom to the people. However, just like us, when the inconvenience passed he went back on his word. How often men and women make promises to God in trouble but when He lovingly hears and delivers them they renounce what they had earlier said.

It is possible that the plague of frogs resulted from their leaving the river due to the pollution of the water. If this is so, the remarkable thing about the plague was that they came and died at the times stated by Moses.

The third plague is described in 8:16–19. It is not clear what the third affliction was. The word used in the original Hebrew language in which the Old Testament was written can mean lice, gnats, mosquitoes or ticks. The last is the most likely. Egypt was used to swarms of insects but it was the timing and the extent of the plague that made this swarm a sign from the Lord.

The important feature of this plague was that 'when the magicians tried to produce ticks by their secret arts, they could not' (v.18). For the first time they are brought face to face with the fact that Moses and Aaron are not doing magical tricks, as, presumably, they thought they had been doing up to this point. As we have already seen, however, they merely explained away what had happened as 'supernatural'. No longer will they compete with Moses and Aaron. Not until 9:11, however, are they completely conquered when the plague of boils strikes them as well!

Questions

1. *God leaves us with more than enough evidence to bring us to faith and to keep it going. Have we ever really considered the evidence available to arouse faith? What might we learn from nature, history, conscience? How might we build our faith on the evidence of Jesus' life and ministry and, above all, His resurrection? What other encouragements to faith can we think of?*

2. *The wonderful activity of God is seldom far out of sight to the believer who looks for it. Do I carefully examine my own circumstances so as to detect God at work? Do I see His hand in the national and international events around me? What practical steps might I take so that my faith can be made stronger by realising that God is at work?*

The Plagues and the gods of Egypt

A connection can be made between most of the plagues and the deities of Egypt. Thus:

Hapi, the god of the Nile, was worshipped as the bringer of fertility (plague 1).

Heq/qet was the frog-headed goddess of fruitfulness (plague 2);

Kepher/a took the form of a beetle (was this included in the 'swarm of flies'?) and symbolised the daily journey of the sun across the sky (plague 4).

Many of the Egyptian gods were depicted as animals (plague 5);

Nut, was the sky goddess who also protected the dead (plague 7);

Seraphia was the protector against the locusts (plague 8);

Re, was the Sun-god, who claimed to be the king of the gods and the father of mankind (plague 9);

Taurt, the goddess of maternity, may lie behind the last plague.

Moreover, Pharaoh, who was finally conquered by the final plague was also believed to be a god.

Exodus 8:20–9:12

The patience of God and the folly of men

Despite God's patience and ever more clear evidence as to who He was, Pharaoh (so typically of unbelievers) refused to acknowledge Him and became ever more stubborn and idiotic in his unbelief.

The first three plagues had been an inconvenience. The next three (8:20–9:12) brought loss and physical suffering. Little by little the Lord increased the pressure.

The first such plague was the swarms of flies (8:20–32). These were probably dog-flies, and would have bitten the Egyptians and stopped all outdoor work. Possibly these flies feasted on the decaying frogs.

It is particularly important to notice verse 22, 'But on that day' said the Lord, 'I will deal differently with the land of Goshen, where my people live; no swarms of flies will be there, so that you will know that I, the Lord, am in this land'. Until this point the plagues seem to have affected the Israelites as well as the Egyptians. From this plague on it is the Egyptians alone who suffer. The Israelites were spared. Before this Pharaoh could have said to Moses and Aaron, 'But if these plagues come from your god, why do your own people also suffer?'. From the fourth plague onwards this excuse could no longer be made.

We have already remarked on the mercy of God shown to the king of Egypt in the plagues. This is so apparent here. God did not need to give Pharaoh ten times to repent. He did not have to place more and more

evidence before Pharaoh. That He did so, emphasises that 'He is patient...,
not wanting anyone to perish, but everyone to come to repentance' (2 Pet
3:9). This tender concern of God is present throughout the plagues.

Instead Pharaoh was willing to allow the people to sacrifice. In 5:4, 17
he had refused this because it would stop the people from working. Now,
with all work stopped, he is willing to allow it: but only if it is closely
supervised by his police force (the point of v.28). This showed that the king
was only willing to concede those things that were forced out of him.
There was no willing acceptance of the will of God and immediately the
danger was removed he once again changed his mind.

We tend to think of Pharaoh as a very wicked man. But maybe he was
no different than we ourselves so often are. His decisions affected the life
of nations. Ours rarely affect more than the few around us. But the reasons
which lie behind our actions are no different from those of Pharaoh. All
too often we will only offer to the Lord those things that He forces out of
us.

Two other plagues quickly followed that of the flies: the plague on the
cattle (9:1–7) and the plague of boils (9:8–12). They seem to have been
intended to re-inforce the challenge of the fourth plague. They had a
similar effect in causing suffering and considerable inconvenience. Sadly,
despite the repeated lesson Pharaoh took no notice. He made no promises,
despite discovering the miraculous nature of the events taking place (v.7).

While it was said in 4:21 that God would harden Pharaoh's heart it is not
until 9:12 that it is said following a plague. This is important. It emphasises
that the Lord's patience was beginning to run out and that judgment was
becoming inevitable. Pharaoh had had many warnings but had become
more and more resistant to the Lord. The time had come for God to
confirm Pharaoh in his folly. How often we, too, put God's patience to the
test. He speaks time and again to us. But the more He speaks to us the less
we take notice. Eventually, we become ripe only for judgment. When the
Lord speaks to us we ought to be like Samuel who said, 'Speak Lord, for
your servant is listening' (1 Sam 3:10). We ought to be quick to listen and
obey.

Questions

1. What lessons may we learn from this passage about rejecting God's message and how might this affect our attitude toward evangelism and mission?

2. God is a patient God, even when handling rebellious people. What evidence do we have to support this truth when we consider our own lives? What comfort may we draw from this fact when we come to Him afresh to seek forgiveness? What can we take from this passage to encourage us?

3. There is a point in our rebellion of God when we put ourselves beyond hope of repentance. Am I sufficiently concerned about those persistent sins in my life? How ought the lessons in my life lead to a change of attitude?

Exodus 9:13–35

Saved to serve

This passage teaches us that God's purpose has always been that He might save His people in order that they might freely obey Him.

The seventh plague is described in 9:13–35: the plague of hail. It is the first of three quite devastating strokes by the Lord against Pharaoh and his people.

This plague is important because of the interpretation it provides and the reason it offers for the Lord wishing the release of His people. Moses first told Pharaoh, 'Let my people go, so that they might worship me' (v.13). In this way God taught that the reason for the deliverance of the people was that they were His. He also emphasised the purpose of the deliverance: 'that they might worship me'.

This remains true of the redemption which Jesus effected. We were saved because we were those upon whom God had placed His love. While we were completely helpless we were saved. Paul teaches this most clearly in Romans 8:29–30. He speaks there of the 'foreknowledge' of God. Some have understood this to mean no more than God's ability to see into the future. Thus, they teach that Paul is saying that God knew in advance who would turn to Him. Those He invited became His children ('called') and, when they received Him, He gave them all the blessings of salvation. Others say that this cannot be what Paul meant. The word 'foreknowledge' does not refer to what God knew but what He did. They feel that this refers to His deliberate plan to save specific people, helpless people. When Paul used the word 'called' in Romans 8 he also meant more than 'invited'. He meant that they were successfully invited. Thus, Paul was teaching the same truth as Exodus 9: God saves helpless people, those unable to help themselves. The bondage of the children of Israel was to Pharaoh. Our bondage is to sin. However, just as the Israelites could not free themselves from Pharaoh, so we are unable to escape from sin. Just as a dead person cannot give himself life, so we cannot do anything to escape from sin. God must and does do it! (see Eph 2:1–10).

Why does God save us? It is to 'worship' Him. For many of us 'worship' is what we do when we meet together with other Christians for a 'service'. For some of us it means a part of the 'service' especially devoted to prayer and praise of God. In fact worship means both of these things: but also far more.

The best word in the English language to express what the Bible means when it speaks of 'worship' is service. Service is the faithful and obedient conduct of a slave to the will of the master or mistress. It speaks of a life wholly devoted to someone else. While both the Bible as a whole and the book of Exodus in particular tell us that we are far more than 'slaves' of God, they do tell us that God expects our service. In the New Testament a different word was often used. That word was 'disciple', but it means the same thing. A Christian is someone who obeys and follows God in everything.

All this is vitally important. We often tend to divide the world of men into three groups: unbelievers, believers and 'saints' or special Christians. 'Saints' are the people who are wholly devoted to God. Believers, we think, are all the other Christians: people whose obedience to the Lord is only partial. In fact, the Bible divides men into only two groups: unbelievers and disciples. We are all called to discipleship or service. Only as we obey do we show the marks of a Christian. If we lack obedience to God, even if we believe all the right things about Jesus, we are still 'unbelievers' because we do not show the distinctive mark of a Christian. This fact ought to be a great challenge to all of us. Do we show by our lives of obedience in every area of our lives that we are real Christians? Or, are we counterfeit? Just as counterfeit money is useless, so counterfeit Christians are both useless and dangerous. They are dangerous, first of all, to themselves because they deceive themselves into thinking that they are secure from God's judgment. They are a danger to others for they encourage others to follow their disastrous example.

The passage in Exodus then tells us two things which we have noticed already. The plagues were also intended to bring Pharaoh to a knowledge of God (v.14) and, because they were repeated, emphasised the great mercy of the Lord (v.15). However, Pharaoh's resistance against God made further judgments inevitable (vv.17,18).

While most of the earlier plagues brought upon the Egyptians disasters that were not unfamiliar to them (though more harshly than usual), hail was and is very unusual in Egypt. The rarity of hail ought to have awakened Pharaoh, once and for all, to the character of his Adversary. He was warring against the one who owned the earth (v.29) and had the right to the service of all. However, though some of his people had been brought to obedience (v.20) this was not true of the king. Thus, though he broke down for the third time (v.27), for the first time acknowledging his sins and those of his people, as well as recognising the righteousness of God, it was a hollow confession. He remained hostile to God.

It is a frightening fact that God sometimes brings people to the point that they experience the horrors of God and yet still will not bow before Him and serve Him. May it happen to none of us!

Questions

1. *What warnings does this passage give to those who do not believe in God? In what way might such teachings be relevant to today?*

2. *True worship involves offering to God the whole of our lives to His service. What difference ought this truth have upon the way we meet with other Christians in 'worship' and how ought it affect our lives?*

3. *God saves the helpless and hopeless. As I reflect upon the lessons taught in this section, what does it do to my pride? And what does it teach me about the mercy and grace of God to me?*

Exodus 10:1–11:10

Building faith and inviting disaster

By persistent rebellion Pharaoh was storing up for himself the inevitable judgment of God against sinners. As with all these chapters, the lessons are there for us to learn too!

The eighth plague, the locust swarm, followed (10:1–20). The story begins, however, with some very important words in verse 2. The Lord told Moses that the people of God were to always tell to the generations which followed them what God had done in Egypt. The reason for this is plain. Nothing encourages faith and obedience more than the recital of the character and purposes of God. All too often believers leave this responsibility to others and neglect to teach these things to their own children. To do so is to disobey a plain command of God.

Few disasters are as devastating as a locust swarm. In countries where locusts sometimes appear a swarm is anticipated with horror. Imagine, then, the unparalleled swarm mentioned here (v.5). However, once again Pharaoh only responded with an easy confession of sin and a shallow repentance which sprang only from a desire to escape the consequences of rebellion. Like Esau before him and many countless persons since 'He could bring about no change of mind, though he sought the blessing with tears' (Heb 12:17). Christian preachers sometimes witness tears in their hearers when they preach the judgment of God. However, when that sense of judgment passes the tears are dried and the hearer's life continues much as before. It is not tears but the changed life that shows true repentance. This was clearly missing in Pharaoh.

The first plague had attacked the power of one of Egypt's greatest gods, the Nile. The ninth plague challenged the other great deity: the sun (10:21–29). The plague of darkness would have been a special insult to Pharaoh: he was believed to be the incarnation of the sun-god.

However, it had no effect on Pharaoh. His offer (v.24) to Moses was a flat refusal to allow the people their freedom, since with their families and livestock still in Egypt the men would have been forced to return. The final judgment was now inevitable.

Moses' words in verse 29 seemed to be wrong. They were rash words spoken in anger. However, they did recognise that the time for discussion had come to an end. They anticipated the horrifying finale of chapter 11.

Until this point in the story each plague has, first, been declared to Moses by the Lord. The description of the actual plague has then followed. This pattern is broken with the final plague. Although it is described in 11:4–8, together with the Israelite plundering of the Egyptians, the events which occur are not actually described until 12:29–36. In between lies the description of the first passover (12:1–28). We shall see how important this is in the discussion below.

No society in the ancient world was more preoccupied with death than that in Egypt. The huge pyramids which still stand today in modern Egypt show this. They emphasise how much time and energy the ancient Egyptians spent in securing a safe passage through death to the life beyond. How severely, then, must the plague of death have affected them!

Of still greater importance is the fact that the Bible writers teach that death is the ultimate and final punishment for sin. Thus, the claim of God to the life of every firstborn Egyptian man was a clear declaration of God that the whole society was under His judgment for sinful rebellion.

Thus, after reminding Moses of His earlier promises (11:1) God proceeds to threaten this horrifying plague upon the Egyptians.

Questions

1. Our faith is strengthened when we remember the activities of God in the past. Do we count and number our own blessings, do we read the great stories of God's mighty acts in the Bible, church history and Christian biography to strengthen our own faith and that of those around us? What steps might we take to strengthen our own faith?

2. Repentance is the fundamental evidence of conversion. As I examine my own life do I find such evidence in me? Or, though I may have shed many tears, do I still live for myself (and my sins) rather than for Jesus? What areas of my life are still closed off from God?

Fig. 1 An illustration from a funeral relief

Exodus 12: 1–28

For all have sinned

The whole world lies under the judgment of God because all have sinned. Even the children of Israel needed God to provide a way that they could escape from His anger and judgment.

Rather strangely the story of the final plague breaks off with the long and detailed description of the instructions for the first celebration of the passover (12:1–28). Unexpectedly, it introduces us to the Israelites as, themselves, under threat of the final plague! It is this which explains why the passover is included at this point: it was given to the Israelites by God Himself as a means of escape from His anger.

No less than Pharaoh, the Israelites had proved to be rebels against the Lord (5:21; 6:9). They had revealed that God's recognition of the sinfulness of mankind (Genesis 6:5) was just as appropriate to them. They were sinners by nature and, inescapably, held in bondage to the gods of Egypt (v.12) who were hostile to God. Two things, then, were required. God must break the power of Egypt and make provision to remove the guilt of the Israelites. Only if He did this could they be His people.

All this explains the vital importance of these verses. The Israelites stood under the wrath of the holy God. The judgment for their sin was death. Before God acted against Egypt it was vital that God do something to remove that verdict. This was provided by the passover ritual.

Fundamental to the ritual was the blood of the lamb (vv.21–23). In the Old Testament blood was thought to symbolise life. This means that the blood of a sacrifice symbolised a life brought to an end by death in a violent way. Often, as here, the blood was seen as substitutionary: that is, it pictured a life given up in the place of another. The life of the firstborn Israelite was due to God: but the life of the lamb was offered in his place. In this way the penalty for sin and the wrath of God was averted (see, especially, v. 23).

The ritual made it very clear that the lamb was to be without defect (v. 5). The Israelites themselves were defective because of their sin. None of them could offer their lives for others because they were under the same judgment. It was necessary that something which symbolised a perfect and sinless life be found. Only such a life given up in death could avert the destroyer (v. 23).

Thus, the passover lamb removed the guilty verdict of God against the Israelites. The penalty for their sin was fully paid and they were free from God's judgment. But that was not all. That same night the power of Egypt over the people was brought to an end.

The passover was also to be celebrated in preparation for a journey (v. 11). Together with the Feast of Unleavened Bread (described in vv. 14–21) this was intended to emphasise that the passover was to mark a *new start*. Leaven or dough is often viewed in the Bible as a symbol of evil. This is obviously true in these verses. Thus, the putting aside of leaven was intended to symbolise lives given over to God in a new start. A break with the past was to be followed by a life of obedience to the Lord.

In the years that followed, these two feasts were to be regularly observed (vv. 24–27) as a permanent reminder of the way in which God had made the Israelites His people. This is emphasised by the fact that the Israelite new year was to be dated from the original passover (v. 1).

And yet it was not all Israelites or even only Israelites who were to benefit from the passover. Earlier, some of the Egyptians had shown respect for the Lord (8:20). Later, a multitude of people, not born Israelites, would accompany the departing descendants of Abraham (12:38). This suggests that many Egyptians must have obeyed God's commands made in this chapter. It was not those who were Israelites by race who proved to be the Lord's people. It was those who obeyed Him.

It is easy to read the Old Testament and think that the Lord was the God of a race. Some of the laws which exclude certain races from joining Israel can be understood in this way (see, for example, Deut 23: 1–8). And yet the laws of ancient Israel were not so much racist as religious. When members of those races became followers of the Lord they were welcomed as full members of His people. This is made especially clear in the Book of Ruth. There one of the Moabite race becomes a follower of the Lord and is made a direct descendant not only of David but 'great David's greater Son'! The people of God in the Bible are only ever truly His when they obey His word.

Questions:

1. *What truth is the most basic one of all which Christians need to communicate to the unbelieving world? Is this consistent with what we teach in our evangelism?*

2. *God saves sinners. As we reflect on these verses, what do they teach us about our own condition (and that of all other men and women)? What can we learn here about the provision that God made for us in Jesus? What sort of response should we make to such knowledge?*

3. *God's salvation brings forgiveness, the removal of guilt and the power to live a new life? Do I believe this or do I still feel unforgiven, guilty and weak? In the light of this passage, what lessons ought I to learn and what steps should I take to ensure I enjoy the full experience of salvation?*

Exodus 12: 29–42

Looking unto Jesus

God covers His people's sin by the provision of the passover lamb. Today, we look to Jesus as the one who died in our place and for our sins.

The Book of Exodus began on tiptoe, looking for the fulfilment of God's promises: promises which centred upon His dealing once and for all with the problem of sin. In the first twelve chapters of Exodus God began to fulfil His word. And yet . . .

Already we have seen that Moses couldn't have been the great leader God had promised in Genesis 3:15. He was a murderer. He pointed forward to someone else and his work anticipated that of someone far greater. In the same way the thoughtful Israelite would have realised that the passover deliverance also pointed into the future to someone or something far greater. He or she would have agreed with the writer to the Hebrews who said, 'it is impossible for the blood of bulls and goats to take away sin' (Heb 10:4). The life of an animal was scarcely a suitable substitute for a man! Like the old man Simeon in the days of Jesus they would have been looking for a man to be the 'salvation' of God (see Luke 2:25–35) and would have eagerly sought the appearing of the one to whom all the ritual pointed.

To what, then, did the passover point? The New Testament also recognises that all are sinners under the death sentence of God (Rom 6:23; 3:23). And the death is not just the physical destruction of the body: it is eternal punishment in hell (Rev 20:13–15). Then it looks from the lamb to *the* Lamb (John 1:29): the spotless God-man who was able to offer up His life as the passover lamb (1 Pet 1:19; 1 Cor 5:7). He broke not the power of Pharaoh, but sin, death and the Devil (Rom 6:6–14). In Him the redeemed are called to a holy life (1 Cor 6:19–20). There is no other escape from God's anger (Acts 4:11–12). Moreover, just as the Israelites had to act upon God's word to benefit from it, so we are called to faith in the Word of God (John 1:1–18, Rom 5:1). Have you faith in Jesus as the only one to deal with your sin?

In chapter 12: 29–36 all that God had promised happened exactly as He said it would. This explains why we are told in detail the events of that night and the following day. The writer of the Book of Exodus does not want us to miss the fact that God is faithful to every word He has spoken. We ought to observe this carefully. The Lord, who is our God, has not changed. Not one word of His will ever fail.

Verses 35–6 have sometimes been misunderstood because the passage has been translated in such a way as to suggest that the Israelites borrowed silver, gold and clothing with no intention of ever giving it back. This was not true. Those versions of the Bible which say that the Israelites *asked* for these items are correct. Doubtless such fear had come upon the Egyptians that they would pay any price to be rid of the children of Israel. This vividly shows how the Lord had powerfully routed those who had held His people powerless. In the New Testament the Lord Jesus has powerfully routed the enemies of God and freed us from the bondage of sin.

Questions

1. *If Jesus is the only way back to God from a life of sin what implications can we draw from our attitude to missionary and evangelistic activity?*

2. *God saves every sort of people. How ought this fact affect our attitudes in evangelism and mission?*

3. *God is faithful to His word even when it seems impossible for Him to achieve what He has promised! As I reflect upon the experience of God's people in Egypt, what can I learn about the way God accomplishes His promises? How ought this affect my confidence and trust in God?*

The Exodus spells freedom

The Book of Exodus has been increasingly used by Christians who, appalled by the injustice they see around them, have supported revolutionary movements for the overthrow of corrupt governments. They say that this story shows that God is on the side of the poor and oppressed and justifies such actions. However, while recognising the difficulties of working out the path of Christian discipleship in such difficult and, often, complicated situations, neither Exodus nor the Bible supports such conclusions.

1) Exodus does not describe a revolution. It describes God's intervention and deliverance of a helpless people. In the story the people do nothing: the Lord does everything. Thus, rather than provide justification for revolutionary change, it offers a picture of a people who patiently wait for God to vindicate them.

2) The Bible is not on the side of the poor but on the side of justice. It is the poor who most often suffer oppression and injustice because they lack power. However, God is never described as being on their 'side'. Wealth and poverty may sometimes be the result of good or bad stewardship. God is not on the side of bad stewards!

3) The Bible consistently teaches that even the worst governments are appointed by Him. This is most clearly stated in Rom 13:1–7 together with the responsibility of believers to be good citizens.

All this does not underestimate the difficulties that believers sometimes find themselves in. Sometimes it is difficult to decide who is the legitimate government. Is it the local guerilla army who hold actual control or is it the national government which claims sovereignty over an area? When and in what way can wicked government demands be resisted – if they can be? For answers to these questions the believer needs the wisdom of God granted by the Holy Spirit. For those of us who are happily free from such difficulties the lesson is that we should be very prayerful for those of our brothers and sisters in Christ who daily have to face such agonising situations.

The Route of the Exodus

In chapters 12–14 various locations are mentioned which are intended to provide us with the route of the Exodus. It began in Rameses and followed the road to Succoth (12:37). From there the Israelites avoided taking the direct route to Canaan (13:17). Thus, leaving Succoth they first camped at Etham (13:20) before turning back to Pi-hahiroth between Migdol and the sea, directly opposite Baal Zephon (14:1–2). From there the people were led through the Red Sea to the Desert of Shur (15:22) and then on to Sinai. Psalm 78:12, 43 adds that the region of Zoan was that from which the people left Egypt.

Three and a half thousand years later it is not easy to reconstruct the route. We can only describe what seems to be most likely.

Rameses, Succoth, Zoan and Shur can be identified with some certainty. Rameses was probably at Khanata-Qantir, a location which would be appropriate for the reign of Amenhotep II. Succoth can probably be identified with Tell el-Maskhutah. Zoan is almost certainly Tanis and Shur is opposite the Bitter Lakes region of Egypt. However, the situations of the other places mentioned are far more difficult to identify and depend upon where the Israelites crossed the Red Sea. On this point there is considerable difference of opinion. Part of the difficulty arises from the name for the sea: the *reed* or *papyrus* sea. Is the name identical to the Red Sea as we know it? It certainly does seem to have included the Gulf of Aqabah and the Gulf of Suez since references in Num 14:25; Deut 1:40; 2:1 and Ex 33:10–11 appear to refer to these two arms of the Red Sea. But could the name be used more generally? Since Egyptians seem to have used geographical names with some freedom it has been suggested that the name could also have applied to the reedy marshes and lakes which ran along a large part of what is now the Suez Canal. It is not impossible that the name could have been used of an arm of Lake Menzelah. It is generally thought that these two locations offer a more likely crossing of the 'Red Sea' than the Gulf of Suez. The favourite location is the Bitter Lakes region of Egypt, especially as Shur is immediately opposite. A further reason is often advanced for this location. In 1945–6 the archaeologist Aly Shafei Bey experienced on a small scale both the strong east winds as described in 14:21 and saw the waters driven back before them.

Certainty on these matters awaits further archaeological discoveries. However, the above suggestion seems the most likely on the present knowledge available.

The Large Number of the Israelites

The figure given in 12:37 suggests that about two and a half million persons left Egypt. This has often been assumed to be unrealistically high and various attempts have been made to explain the Bible text. It has to be admitted that the text of the Hebrew Scriptures has preserved numbers badly (compare the numbers in parallel passages in Kings and Chronicles). Extra 'noughts' could have been added. Also, we are told in other passages of the fewness of the people (Deut 4:38; 7:7,17,22). It is also true that the average population of a town in the ancient world was only 5,000. However, if the 70 descendants of Jacob had been in Egypt for over 400 years and had been blessed by the Lord with a large increase in numbers, it is not difficult to take the figure here seriously. Moreover, migrations of enormous numbers of people are recorded in ancient history and 38:26; Num 1:46; 2:32 and 11:21 seem to confirm the accuracy of the figure here.

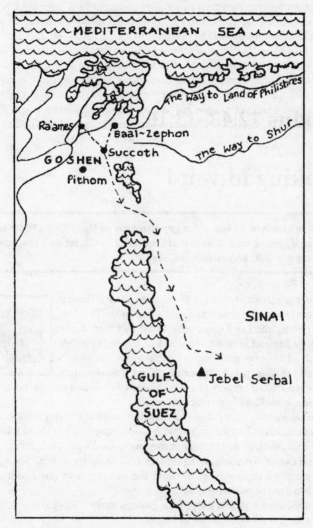

Map 1: The route of the exodus from Egypt

Exodus 12:43–13:16

Looking forward

The Israelites had to show the genuineness of their claim to be God's children by the obedient lives that they led. The Christian's responsibility to live for God is certainly no less!

The last verses of chapter 12 (43–51) introduce a further regulation about the observance of the passover. This law was probably the Lord's response to the fact that 'many people' (v.38) had joined themselves to the descendants of Jacob. The new situation explains why the law is included at this point. In future, God commanded, nobody was to celebrate or share in the passover unless the male members of his household had been circumcised.

We have already learnt that circumcision was the act which symbolised that an individual had identified with God's people. Only those who had visibly indicated, in this way, that they were God's people were to share in the passover. This is easy to understand. Only those who were truly God's people had any right to claim the privileges of His children, as symbolised in the passover meal.

The final verses in this part of the Exodus story (13:1–16) record some more of the Lord's commands to Moses.

They begin with instructions about the Feast of Unleavened Bread (vv.3–10). The feast symbolised the 'new start' of God's people and their commitment to Him in a life of obedience. The instructions about the consecration of the firstborn (vv.1,2,11–16) were intended to make the same point. This explains why the two practices are interwoven and linked together in this passage. The firstborn had been spared by God and were to be devoted to Him. But they symbolised the whole people of God under judgment. Thus, their 'consecration' was a public reminder that *all* Israel were the Lord's and were called to obedient service.

Once again the Book of Exodus teaches us that we are saved to serve. It is a theme which runs throughout the book and unites all its different parts. Saved from sin we are to serve the Lord. It is popular today for Christian writers and preachers to challenge professing believers to accept the lordship of Jesus as a second stage of Christian discipleship. It is understandable why this is done. So many people who say they are Christians do not *live* as though they are what they claim. But in the Bible, salvation and obedience go together. Obedience is the reflex action of the person who has been saved. Thus it is not so much the case that people need to recognise Jesus' lordship as to be called to true and not counterfeit Christianity. The challenge to disobedient professing Christians must be far more radical than it usually is. Such people are not to be called to a more committed Christian life. They are to be called to repentance and true faith!

It is important to notice that God, once again, stresses the responsibility of the people to teach those who follow them (vv.8,14–16). This family responsibility is widely applied in the New Testament. For example, Christian leaders are to instruct others (Titus 1:9) and older women are to teach and equip others (Titus 2:3–5). The Christian church has, all too often, been found to harbour doctrinal error and (the inevitable consequence) moral indiscipline. Sadly, this suggests that the importance of 'making disciples' has been sadly neglected. Content with people who claim Christian faith we have not been prepared to help them grow to maturity.

Before we leave these verses we need to notice one further important truth. God's instructions in these verses repeatedly remind the people that the deliverance from bondage was not the final goal of His people (vv.5,11). It was the prospect of the land which was to strengthen the people and drive them on through the desert. That land would 'flow with milk and honey' (v.5). In the ancient world this would have meant two things. It would have been seen as a reference to paradise and the place where the gods lived. For Israel it pointed to Eden restored: to the place where God's people would enjoy His presence in a world free from the curse of sin.

Canaan never quite lived up to the dreams of the Israelites. And for a very good reason. As with so many of the places, people and events of the Old Testament the land pointed forward. It anticipated the time when the curse for sin would be finally removed and the Creation itself would be restored to its original purpose. One day God would restore the world so that it would glorify God and provide the place in which men and women would be able to delightedly serve the Lord. Romans 8, especially verses 8–12, speaks about this.

The Lord Jesus has come and has finally dealt with the guilt of sin and has broken its power. However, we are still expected to eagerly await the time of His return. And it is the hope of fellowship with Him, unhindered by all the consequences of sin, which is to be our motivation as Christians. Just as an athlete trains hard in order to win some future prize, so we are to set this delightful hope before us. Yet how often we lose sight of the goal! How often we think of Christianity in terms of the benefits which we can gain now! We need to remember the words of the writer to the Hebrews, when he said, 'They did not receive the things promised; they only saw and welcomed them from a distance. And they admitted that they were aliens and strangers on earth. People who say such things show that they are looking for a country of their own. If they had been thinking of the country they had left, they would have had opportunity to return. Instead, they were longing for a better country – a heavenly one. Therefore, God is not ashamed to be called their God' (Heb 11:13–16).

Questions

1. Sometimes the world seems full of people who say they are Christians but they do not seem to live as Christians. What might this passage have to say to such people?

2. Salvation is confirmed by our receiving the covenant sign. Have I been baptised and, if not why not if I claim to be a Christian?

3. A true believer is living for the future. As I consider my own life can I really say this is true for me? In what ways is it not true? What things stop me from living as I should? How might I take steps to put this right?

Exodus 13:17–14:31

Short memories

The God who had stood by His people in the past is here revealed as the Lord who is with them in their present. Faithless and doubting though the Israelites proved to be, the Lord did not fail them; nor will He fail us!

An experienced man or woman may be able to cross a desert and find the way with some certainty. But the person who is not used to such terrain will find it bewildering and will easily become lost. This was the danger that now stood before the Israelites. It is a danger that we face as we step out in the way of discipleship.
What we need was given to the Israelites: the assured presence of God (13:21–2). For them the visible symbol of the presence of the invisible God was provided. To us He has given His word: the completely reliable guide to our faith and our conduct. He has also given us His Spirit so that we can wisely discern the will of the Lord. Thus, like Israel of old, we can go out into the unknown future with the certain confidence that we can trust Him.

Organised as they were (v.18) the people were also untrained and inexperienced. Today, national governments know that the best soldier is the trained one. Faced with severe difficulty he will prove his worth while the inexperienced man will crumble under lesser stresses. The God of Israel understands the nature of man better than anyone else. Hence, though less than a week would have brought the people to the borders of Canaan He found it necessary as a result of their weakness and sin to lead them out into the desert for forty years before they were ready for the warfare of conquest (vv.17–18). There is a comforting lesson here. The apostle Paul recognised this when he said, 'He will not let you be tempted beyond what you can bear. But when you are tempted, He will also provide a way out so that you can stand up under it' (1 Cor 10:13). Sometimes Christian preachers seek to challenge their hearers' faith by quoting an example of Christian faithfulness under the severest trial. This is understandable but not really fair. What we need is not the guarantee that we will be able to face such situations in the unlikely event that we may be tried in the same way. Rather we need the confidence that where we are, in our daily walk with the Lord, He will be with us and protect us. This assurance the Bible gives us both by example and direct word from the Lord.

In verse 19 we are reminded of the confidence of Joseph in Genesis 50:24,25. He had been assured that God would be faithful to His promises. Thus, he had commanded the Israelites to take his body with them when they left Egypt. God had now begun to reward Joseph's faith. As a result his bier would be a permanent reminder of the faithfulness of God to His word through all the wanderings in the desert. But if Joseph had had to wait 400 years the Israelites would only have to wait forty!

Modern Christians show a remarkable lack of interest in Church history and in the faithfulness of God to believers of past generations. The result is that, very often, the people of God are crippled by a lack of faith and vision. Not so the Israelites. They would have been strengthened by Joseph's faith.

The lessons of these early verses are vividly illustrated in the events which immediately followed: the crossing of the Red Sea (14:1–31). Persuaded by the apparently confused course which the Israelites were taking that they could be easily subdued and returned to their former duties, Pharaoh decided to gather the powerful might of his army together to attack the people of God. Everything appeared to be against them: desert on the one side, the sea on the other and Pharaoh approaching from the only possible way of escape!

We can well imagine the terror of the people. They were a group of ill-equipped men and women faced with the greatest military might of the ancient world! Their response was understandable and human (14:10). They cried out to the Lord and they criticised Moses, thus showing their lack of confidence in both Moses and their God. Despite the fact that the Lord had told Moses (and he presumably had told them) exactly what was happening they reacted with fear. Perhaps, like us, the new experience left them with the uncomfortable feeling, 'Can our God really cope?'. Like many a Christian leader Moses assured the people, despite the fact that he, too, was reaching the limits of his faith (vv.13–15). And yet his words provided the key to the whole situation. They offered the only hope that they could possibly have, 'Do not be afraid. Stand firm and see the deliverance the Lord will bring you today' (v.13).

The sequel is well known. At a command from Moses the sea divided and the people went over on dry ground (vv.21–2). Meanwhile they were protected by the Lord from the rear (vv.19–20) and then the army of Egypt was destroyed without the Israelites doing anything at all (vv.23–28)!

The result is as briefly stated as it is inevitable. 'The Lord saved Israel...the people feared the Lord and put their trust in Him and in Moses His servant' (vv.30–1). The fear had been unnecessary and the victory certain.

Like Israel we find this a difficult lesson to learn. Yet when learned it is the source of great peace and joy even in the most difficult circumstances.

Significantly, we read that Moses said, 'the Egyptians you see today you will never see again' (v.13). This probably helps explain why the New Testament seems to reflect this incident in the language it uses about baptism. It is a symbol of the power of sin broken in death and life released to be freely given to the Lord (Rom 6:1–4). Do we live in a way that proves our testimony in baptism to be true?

Questions

1. *God's training, testing and equipping of His people is always designed to ensure that we are ready to face the challenges of life as obedient disciples. As we think carefully about this passage and our own experience what evidence can we find to show that this statement is true?*

2. *God's past dealings with His people are designed to reassure us; He is the same yesterday, today and forever. What might I do to ensure that my own past experience and that of God's people down the ages is a reassurance to me in my daily life of discipleship?*

Exodus 15:1–21

Joyful stewardship

God's mighty deliverance of His people caused Moses to break forth into joyful song which celebrated the presence of God in the midst of His people. Today the same truth should fill us with joy too!

Throughout the world, excitement and joy overflow into song. So the Israelites burst forth into praise to God for the great deliverance at the Red Sea (15:1,20–21). Today song remains an important evidence of a people alive to the blessings of God. If Christians do not worship can they really claim to have understood what great things God has done for them?

Moses' song may be divided into two halves. In verses 1–12 he celebrated the great deliverance which the children of Israel had so recently experienced. Then in verses 13–18 he confidently described what the Lord would go on to do for His people. These two halves are closely linked together. What God had done revealed His true character. He was quite different and altogether more majestic than any human rival. This was established by what He had done (vv.11–12). Knowing this and the promises of God secured the future blessing of the people of God.

In his response to the blessing of God, Moses set an example for us all. We, too, are expected to search our own experience for evidence of the hand of the Lord. In particular, we are to watch carefully for answers to prayer. In this way our confidence in God will be increased. We will observe how our experience confirms His character as revealed in the Bible. Armed with His promises we shall also be able to face the future confident that the Lord will fulfil His word and prove to be One who does not change: who is the same yesterday, today and forever.

The mention of 'your holy dwelling', 'the mountain of your inheritance' and 'the sanctuary' (vv.13,17) may refer to the city of Jerusalem or the Temple mount. It is, however, more likely a reference to the land of Canaan as a whole. In the imagery of the ancient world the gods were thought to live high on a distant mountain, far away from their people. A sanctuary was, however, a place where they were, in some way, present. These ideas seem to lie behind Moses' words.

The entire land was the Lord's sanctuary and the land itself was the 'mountain' where He dwelt. The Lord was no distant god uninterested in the affairs of His people. He lived in the midst of them!

This truth would prove to have two sides to it. On the one hand the people could live secure in the fact that the Lord was ever on hand to help them and they could always enjoy fellowship with Him: just as Adam and Eve had in the Garden of Eden. The land was to be a 'heaven on earth'.

On the other hand the land was never absolutely theirs. It was the Lord's and was entrusted to them as tenants. That tenancy could be lost through failure to live as His people. Because of the presence of sin among the people this would always be a real threat and, one day, they would lose the land when they were taken away in exile. This weakness pointed forward to the time when sin would be finally dealt with. It showed that the land symbolised something far greater. One day God would so deal with sin that His people would enjoy all the blessings of fellowship with God but without the danger of the blessing being lost through sin. As believers we look for a 'new Jerusalem' in which this great hope will be finally realised (see Rev 21:1–4; 22:1–5).

Before we leave these verses we need to notice the further repetition of God's goodness (v.19 and compare 14:21–22,29). God's salvation was so marvellous to the author of the book of Exodus that he kept returning to the same theme and rejoicing in it. May we never lose sight of the marvel of our salvation and always find something in it to excite our wonder and praise as well as arouse our desire to share it with others.

Questions

1. *Is the fact that we joyfully declare that God has saved us the one thing that strikes the watching world? If not, why not?*

2. *Those things that God reveals of Himself in the Bible are intended to give us great joy. What truths have been taught us in this passage and our recent experience? How can we use these truths in such a way as to encourage us?*

3. *Everything that we have and are we have as stewards of God. Thinking about the various gifts, abilities and privileges I have, how well am I stewarding what God has given to me?*

Exodus 15:22–27

Difficulty and disappointment

Israel begins to learn the fact that following the Lord is often far from easy and demands humble trust and faithful obedience even when the going 'gets tough'.

After the remarkable rescue from bondage and the miracle of the Red Sea the people of God had testified to their trust in the Lord (14:31) and confessed their confidence in Him (15:13), especially as the God able to do things beyond every imagination (15:11–12). The victorious progress of the people through the desert to the land of Canaan seemed to be assured. However, the path of faithful obedience to the Lord is never quite as simple as that. This new section of Exodus illustrates the point.

Only three days journey from the point where they had crossed the Red Sea the people encountered their first difficulty (v.22). They experienced the minor inconvenience of finding a water supply which had a bitter, but not poisonous, taste. This is not uncommon in desert water supplies fed from artesian wells. The response of the people was both immediate and tragic. They complained against Moses and, by implication, his God.

Someone once said, 'It is a very common experience that the joy of conversion, of a living contact with Christ, often turns to deep disappointment as unexpected difficulties are encountered'. We do not find it easy to grasp that difficulties are part of God's loving training (Heb 12:3–11) and it is all too easy for Christian preachers to depict the Christian life in a way which leaves little room for 'suffering with Christ'. This was a lesson the

Israelites needed to learn. The fact that God was fully able to meet their needs by remarkable and miraculous deeds was not intended to imply that He would not sometimes severely test their faith in order to bring them to maturity. The sad thing was (and is) that God's people found it difficult to cope with even the most minor inconvenience. An insignificant difficulty was in danger of completely wrecking their discipleship. How often is this true with us.

Yet not only was God able to fully meet the situation (v.25) but the waters of Elim were probably only 6 or 7 miles away. This is usually the case in God's dealings with us. Difficulties there are. But times of comfort and peace are seldom far away.

But the people's disobedience did lead to a warning from the Lord (vv.25–26). In Egypt the people had been spared the worst of the plagues. The judgment of God upon the Egyptians had by-passed the Israelites. However, the same God who had spared them would judge them, too, if they persisted in faithlessness. The same sort of judgments that He had brought against the Egyptians would be their experience too.

There is a persistent tendency among Christians to think that to claim to be one of the Lord's children is enough to secure them from the judgment of God. This was never true. God expects His children to follow Him faithfully: to show a family likeness to Him. If they fail to do so they show that they are not His children and have no part of the blessings of His family.

Questions

1. God is judge. How should this make a difference to our evangelism?

2. God is our father; thus, He loves and disciplines us. Do we presume upon God's love? Are we surprised when God seems to be rebuking us? What does this passage teach us about God to govern our attitude toward God?

3. God is greater than all circumstances. Have I learnt this lesson which the Israelites seemed so slow to understand? What circumstances and experiences in my life seem too big for Him? How can I apply the lessons of this passage to those situations?

Exodus 16:1–17:16

God's faithfulness and man's unfaithfulness

Learning to be disciplined and uncomplaining is not easy for human beings. Israel failed their early tests of obedience, as, so often, do we. Yet God was merciful to them!

Chapter 16:1–36 describes a further trial which God placed before the Israelites. Inconvenience at Marah was succeeded by lack in the desert of Sin. Egyptian slaves were generally well looked after. That Israel had known that is implied in 16:3. Doubtless the pleasures of the past were exaggerated: but that is so often the way. What was remarkable was that less than three months after the people had been delivered from cruel bondage they were complaining that the menu in the desert was not good enough! For that was the point. Whatever they might have said about starving the reality was that they had left Egypt with their flocks and herds (12:38).

We are no different. Losing sight of the greatness of all that God has and is doing for us we become discouraged because we think God ought to be doing better. We shortsightedly focus on a minor lack and lose sight of the vast treasures that are ours in Christ Jesus.

In the passage the folly of the people is forcefully stated. They had grumbled (v.2) and that grumbling had been against the Lord (vv.7,8,9,11). The very God who had faithfully provided Abraham, Isaac, Jacob and, most remarkably, them was the object of their complaints. What a rebuke to us when we react to inconvenience or lack in the same way!

Amazingly, God gave them what they wanted *and* made arrangements for their long-term need for food. First came the quail and then the provision of manna (vv.13–15). Each were given as evidence that the Lord would always provide for His people (v.12). In our own faithlessness God is often far more merciful than we deserve.

And yet we so often react exactly as many of the Israelites did. Given detailed instructions by the Lord concerning the collection of manna (vv.15–16,23) and evidence that they would receive all that they needed (vv.17–18) there were still those who persistently disregarded His words (vv.20,27). And the only people to lose as a result of such conduct were those who disobeyed. It is so easy to be deceived (as Adam and Eve were) into thinking that God's commands are for His benefit and not ours. Sadly, the world is full of people whose lives have been scarred or even wrecked because they think in this way. We need to discipline ourselves to recognise that all that the Lord requires of us is for our blessing and good.

The last verses of chapter 16 contain a repeated reference to the pot of manna which was to be subsequently stored in the ark of the Testimony. This should have provided the people with a permanent reminder that the Lord gives His people each day 'their daily bread'. The following chapters show, however, how often this was ignored or forgotten.

Two further trials are described in chapter 17: the lack of water (17:1–7) and the attack of the Amalekites (17:8–16). Sometimes the believer finds himself in a situation which is disastrous: unless, that is, God intervenes. That was true for Israel when they came to Rephidim. Unlike Marah, where the water had been bitter but drinkable, at Rephidim there was no water at all. Immediately, the people assumed the worst of the Lord (v.7). Their question implies that they doubted His ability to meet this need. Despite their doubts the Lord did provide (vv.5,6). Indeed, it is interesting to notice that the name given to the place did not reflect His provision but the doubts of the people. God's provision was entirely predictable. What was more remarkable was the response of the people and it was that response that gave the names 'Testing' and 'Quarrelling' to the place.

The Christian very soon learns that the path of true discipleship is beset with warfare. Sin and the Devil are not easily conquered and battle characterises even the youngest believer. John understood this. In his first letter he told the 'young men' that they had overcome the evil one (2:13,14). Whatever else could be said of them they had experienced and gained some victories in Christian warfare. Thus, we are not surprised by the attack of the Amalekites against the Israelites. Nor should we be surprised that the victory was won through prayer. To stand with uplifted arms is still the posture of prayer in many parts of the world. It was in the ancient world. Thus Moses prayed and Joshua won the victory over the enemy of God's people (v.14).

The last two verses are not easy to understand. However, it is probable that the thought is that Moses declares that under the Lord's banner victory is assured. The Lord is no less the banner of the New Testament believer.

These chapters are surely intended to teach us all that difficulties and trials are to be seen as tests (15:25; 16:4) intended to lead us to daily trust in the Lord (see, especially chapter 16), to obedience (16:20,27) and prayer (17:10–13). In this way, and this way alone, we can arrive at mature discipleship.

We are also shown the mercy of God. Time and again the people failed the test but the Lord was gracious to them. But we cannot presume upon that mercy. Later the people would be tested again in almost identical ways (Numbers 20:12; 11:33; 14:25). However, failure then led to the exclusion of Moses from Canaan, many slain by a plague from the Lord and to the victory of the same Amalekites. Many failed, in this way, to enter the promised salvation rest of God in the land (see Heb 3:7–13). The warning to us is obvious!

Questions

1. God helps to make us mature through giving us difficulties to test us. When we consider our present problems how well are we coping with them? Are they disrupting our walk with God or enriching it and producing maturity?

2. Spiritual warfare is inevitable for the Christian. Am I surprised at the difficulties I encounter as a Christian? If so, why? What may I learn from this passage which will assist me to have a proper understanding of the spiritual warfare involved in the life of discipleship? What are the areas in which I have to battle? How may I have success?

Exodus 18:1–27

Servants together

Israel begins to see the effect of their deliverance as others come to know their God. They also discover some of the basic lessons of successful leadership. Such lessons may be 'down to earth' but they are always relevant and important.

At this point in the account of the people's journey to Sinai there is a surprising break. Before the people arrive at the mountain of God we are told the story of Jethro's visit to his son-in-law Moses. This hardly seems important enough to give it more than a brief mention. And yet a whole chapter is given over to a detailed recital of the visit!

However, there are two very good reasons why this story was included. First of all it was important to the writer of Exodus that the words of Jethro's confession be recorded (vv.9–12). Israel had been called to be a blessing to the nations (Gen 12:3). Through God's salvation of them many others were to come to know the Lord. Thus, we are told of Jethro's confession. It was intended to remind Israel of their great calling and was recorded as a pattern of the profession of many who, through Israel, would come to know and trust in the Lord.

In the New Testament the great purpose of the Church is unchanged. Jesus commanded His disciples, 'Go into all the world and make disciples'. He assured them that He would bless them as they faithfully obeyed Him. 'I will be with you always', He said (Matt 28:18–20). A Christian or church which does not have this aim falls far short of the calling of God. Yet a people who are to be a witness to the world need to be organised in such a way as to ensure that the work is done as well as it is possible to do it. The people of God are not a group of individuals who all do what they think is best. They are a people who *together* will achieve far more than they can as individuals.

But the question remains as to how the people can be best organised to achieve God's purposes for them. This is the point of the second half of the chapter (vv.13–27). Interestingly, it was a wise but recently converted man who was the one through whom the Lord revealed His will for Israel. Jethro's experience taught him that Moses' approach to leadership was quite wrong. Common sense showed that it could only lead to disaster for the people of God. All too often Christians adopt practices in the church which a little common sense would show up as silly. Sadly, common sense seems to be a rare thing among the people of God!

Jethro recognised that though God had richly blessed His people (vv.9,10) the dependence of Israel on one man for their leadership was a dangerous and wrong thing (v.17). He gave three reasons for this. Firstly, he recognised that such practices placed too much strain upon the one leader (v.18). Secondly, he saw that the needs of the whole people would not be best met if one person was responsible to meet them all (v.14). Finally, he pointed out that the gifts which God had given to His people were not being used for the benefit of one another (vv.19–23).

When we come to the New Testament we find the same principles are to govern the Church. We are given clear teaching that the leadership in a local church is to be in the hands of a number of people (Acts 20:17; Phil 1:1; Acts 14:23; Jas 5:14). Detailed instructions, like those given by Jethro to Moses, are given as to who should be appointed leaders (see, especially, 1 Tim 3:1–7). Yet every member of the church has God-given gifts (1 Cor 12:7,11). All are called to use their gifts to the benefit of one another (1 Thess 5:11,14).

All this *really is* common sense. After all, when men and women work together they work best as a team where each person uses his or her own abilities as best they can, helped by a good leadership. Jethro understood this: but few Christians seem to share his wisdom. Frequently, even leaders themselves suggest that leadership of a local church is best undertaken by one person. The teaching and the care of the members of the church are that person's 'job'. Often this leader is thought to have some special 'calling' quite different from the calling of all other Christians. The result of this is that many Christian leaders have to bear very heavy burdens while the rest of the people do little or nothing. When the weight becomes too heavy and the leader collapses under the weight, God's people are sympathetic. But they rarely realise that it is they *themselves* who are responsible. They continue to complain when anything goes wrong in the life of the church and blame the leader. They expect the leader to do things which they have no right to expect of him.

At the same time God's people often find it difficult to believe that they have gifts which the church needs just as much as those of leadership. Sometimes they are not encouraged to find out what gifts they have and are not trained or helped. Leaders sometimes feel threatened by other active members! But there is no doubt what the Bible's pattern is: and there is every evidence available to show the wisdom of its teachings.

Many of us will, however, continue to ignore what the Bible teaches. After all, it is far easier if someone else does all the work and takes all the responsibility. When we do this, however, we need to realise what we are doing. We are unfairly treating our leaders. We are depriving fellow believers: we are stealing from them by not sharing our gifts with them. We are harming the cause of the Gospel because many can do what a few can never achieve. In the end we are a danger to ourselves. Disobedience finds its fruit in rejection by Jesus.

Questions

1. *Are there any reasons that we can think of which might explain why people today are less impressed with the people of God than Jethro was?*

2. *God saves His people in order that they might be witnesses. As I consider my own life do I consistently witness by the way I live? Am I committed (and is my church) to witnessing for Jesus at every available opportunity?*

3. *God equips all His people so that, together, they can serve Him. Are we the sort of Christians who leave everything to others? Or, do we think that we are the only ones who know how to do a good job well? What lessons ought we to learn from this passage of Scripture?*

Exodus 19:1–25

The loving obedience of holy children

Israel is encouraged to rest unconditionally in the love of God and serve Him in delighted obedience. We are expected to do the same, especially in the light of God's love which has been shown to us in Jesus.

Chapter 19 begins a new section of the Exodus story (19:1–24:12). The Lord had delivered the people from Egypt, where they had served Pharaoh. Now they were to serve Him. In these chapters the nature of the relationship which He had planned to exist between Himself and the people is revealed.

Chapter 19 is perhaps one of the most important chapters in the Bible. Some of the most basic lessons of the Scriptures are contained within its 25 verses. We need to give careful attention to all that is taught here.

After arriving at Sinai, just as the Lord had promised (3:12), Moses was called up to the top of the mountain where God intended to reveal Himself (vv.1–3). There the Lord reminded Moses that the salvation of Israel was the result of His grace and tenderness. When young eagles begin to fly, the mother eagle hovers around and beneath them and is ready to give support on her outstretched wings to the weak and tired. It is by this picture that the Lord chose to teach Moses about what He had done for Israel. Throughout the earlier chapters of Exodus it was God who had intervened to save His helpless people (see, especially, 3:8). He had done this despite their frequent acts of stubbornness (5:21; 6:9; 16:3; 17:2 etc.).

Tenderly and without thought for what they deserved He had saved them (v.4).

Paul teaches that the salvation of the New Testament believer in Jesus is no different. Without any ability to save ourselves we were helpless and under the judgment of God. But in our weakness and sin all the resources were given to us to welcome Jesus: even our faith (Eph 2:1–10). Praise Him!

But if salvation is all of grace it should lead to total obedience to God (v.5). There is an apparent contradiction here. How, we ask, can a God who saves entirely by grace then require obedience as the basis for giving His salvation? But there is no difficulty. Salvation is by grace. But the evidence of salvation is seen in obedience. Thus, to claim salvation and not obey is to show that God's grace has never been truly experienced.

The obedience of the people of God is to be without any qualification. In the ancient world a victorious king would state the terms upon which his people were to serve him. They could not negotiate with him: only obey. The Israelites were placed by the Lord in a similar situation. He could demand of them whatever He wished. But this was not the complete story. He claimed total obedience because He had redeemed them. God had done for them more than they could have ever hoped. The only possible response could be loving obedience. And obedience affected by love is a delight not a duty!

This same lesson is taught in the New Testament. God so loved the world that He sent His own Son to be our saviour (John 3:16). We love Him because He first loved us (1 John 4:19) and in delighted obedience find that His burden is easy to carry because it is borne in love (Matt 11:29–30). The mark of our maturity as believers is seen when we obey Jesus not because we must but because we want to.

It is interesting that all this is emphasised by the fact that the Israelites were called to obey and agreed to do so (v.8) before God had shown any of His will to them. That would follow in chapters 20–24. God's salvation of them should have given them enough confidence to offer themselves completely to Him. So God's love shown in the giving of His Son should be sufficient to give us confidence that what is entrusted to Him will be treated with the utmost love. It has been said that much of the disappointment in many a Christian life goes back to an unwillingness to rest unconditionally in His love.

If the Israelites thought that such a claim over them was harsh then that opinion must have been removed by the Lord's next words (vv.5,6). It was not as slaves that they were called to serve Him. No slave was ever the 'treasured possession' of his master. The language of the Lord was far more that of the family, for Israel was the firstborn son of the Lord (4:22). No less is true of us if we are Christians (Gal 4:7). And if we are sons it is

God's purpose that He share with us all the riches of His glory. No less is ours if we are His treasured possession.

In addition to this, Israel were given the greatest possible calling. They were to be a 'kingdom of priests'. This meant that they were to have the privilege of bringing a knowledge of God to the lost, sinful world.

Finally, they were promised that they would be a 'holy nation'. God would remake them so that the character and the blessings of Adam and Eve in the Garden of Eden would be theirs. For us there is little appeal in being holy. The reason for this is that we tend to think of holiness as a life deprived of the things we most enjoy! But holiness in the Bible is a lovely thing. It is reflecting the beauty and loveliness of God Himself. It leads to the enjoyment of His fellowship and blessing. When we meet a truly holy Christian there is something delightful and attractive in them. It was this privilege that was held out before the Israelites.

All these privileges are applied to believers in the New Testament (1 Pet 2:9–10). May we prove worthy of them and in obedience find the assurance they bring that we are His.

Though they often departed from their profession in the days which followed, it is, nevertheless to the people's credit that they willingly offered their obedience (v.8). The verses that follow emphasise, however, that the Lord was not content with mere words. Confession was to be followed by obedient actions. In addition to this the Lord displayed His unapproachable holiness. Thus, God's tenderness and love was not to lead to over-familiarity or indiscipline. He was and is no less a holy God than He is the God of love. This great truth is, above all, displayed in the Cross of Jesus. The Cross was a mighty display of the love of God for sinners. But it was also a clear statement that God hates sin. The marvellous thing is that His love exhausted His wrath on the Cross. Nevertheless, we, too, are called to a life of faith and holy actions (Jas 2:17).

Questions

1. The picture of the true believer in God that we find in this chapter is a very attractive one. Is this the picture that we display to the watching world?

2. Christians are called to love God and serve Him willingly with everything they have and are. Have we learnt to freely serve God and delight to follow His will because He loves us and we love Him? What steps might we take to increase our love? Are there lessons we could learn from this chapter?

3. Christians are expected to enjoy the privileges of the children of God. What picture do I have of God and His relationship with me? Do I enjoy the intimacy of knowing that He is my father and I am His child? What might I learn from this passage of my Father's love for me? Do I believe it?

Exodus 20:1–21

The God who is to be neither shared nor manipulated

God expects from His people that their wholehearted love for Him will be matched by their love to all other men and women that He has made.

Chapter 19 showed the response God expected of the Israelites who had experienced His salvation. Both in their words and their actions they were to show delighted obedience to the Lord. The question must naturally have followed: 'What does the Lord want us to do?'. Chapters 20:1–24:12 are an account of the answer which God gave.
First of all (20:1–17) the basic principles which were intended to govern all their conduct was revealed by God. Then, an explanation of how these principles were to apply to particular situations was given (20:18–24:12). This 'charter' is a lot shorter than similar law codes in the ancient world. This suggests that the laws were given as examples of how to apply the moral principles revealed by God to other situations.

The introduction to the Ten Commandments (vv.1,2) is important for two reasons. First of all, we are plainly taught that the words came from God, the King. His will, reflecting His own character, was revealed in these commands which were not subject to negotiation. They were sovereign demands which had to be obeyed. Secondly, we are reminded of the theme which was so prominent in chapter 19. These laws were given to Israel as those who had already enjoyed the salvation of God. Thus, these laws were never intended (as so many Christians seem to believe) to provide a standard for salvation by personal effort. Rather, they were given to a people already redeemed as the standard expected of a life now devoted to God. In this respect the New Testament is no different. We, too, are called to detailed obedience to the will of God. While for us the standard of obedience has shifted from the words of God to the Word of God there is no suggestion that the words of God have lost their relevance (Matt 5:20). Our salvation from sin, the salvation to which the deliverance from Egypt could only point, provides an incentive to closer faithfulness to God and the power which alone can effect true obedience (Rom 8:3,4).

The Ten Commandments can be divided into two groups. The first four point out the duty of the Israelites to the Lord. The last six describe their responsibilities to one another. However, we should be careful that we do not think that one part of the list is more important than the other. Christians often give the impression that the duties to God were more important. Unbelievers tend to regard the moral duties to one another as all important. In fact the ten laws went together. Thus, the demand of God for the devotion of His people went together with His demand for caring conduct among the people. In the New Testament we find the same emphasis. We are to love God because He first loved us. Then we are to love one another as a proof that we truly do love God. And the standard of our love is nothing less than the love of Jesus for sinners (1 John 4:19 and John 13:34–5).

The first four commandments were intended to teach the Israelites that God expected total, wholehearted obedience and dedication to Him. The first commandment emphasised this by requiring the people to never share their allegiance to the Lord with anyone or anything else (v.3). It was rarely a temptation to the Israelites to give up the Lord in exchange for another god. They were always, however, in danger of dividing their devotion between Him and others. Thus, as Christians we are seldom inclined to give up our faith in God. What we all too often do, however, is to allow other people or things to gradually take the place in our lives which should be occupied only by the Lord. When we do this we are not walking faithfully before God.

The second commandment is recorded in verses 4–6. To understand it we need to know that in the ancient world (and in parts of the modern world) access to an image of a god was thought to give the worshipper some control over the god. It enabled the god to be manipulated. This explains why the Israelites were never permitted to make any image of the Lord. He was and is a God who is unable to be manipulated by men. The prophet Isaiah illustrated this when he said, 'Lebanon is not sufficient for altar fires, nor its animals enough for burnt offerings (to manipulate Him)' (40:16). In the time of the prophet Lebanon was covered by the most luxuriant forest in the known world and supported the most remarkable variety of wild life. The prophet taught that even if all the animals were sacrificed on a bonfire made of all the trees, God could not be manipulated. This is the point which the second command was intended to make.

We tend to follow God because of what we think we shall be able to get out of Him. We serve Him selfishly. The second command was intended to teach the people of Israel that He is to be served because of who He was and what He had done. What a difference there would be in our worship and service of God if this was the motive which governed all that we do! Yet if this was required of the Israelites nothing less is required of us who have known the Word of God who 'lived for a while among us' (John 1:14).

Questions

1. Non Christians often think they have to do something to please God. What answer does this passage give to such ideas?

2. The worship and service of the Lord is not to be shared with anyone or anything else. We might not be tempted to desert God but what people and things are in danger of sharing the place in our lives which is truly His? In what ways could our ambitions, families, hobbies, homes, jobs etc. become 'gods'?

3. The Lord cannot be manipulated by men and women. Why do I serve God? Is it in order to get what I want out of life and Him? Or, do I serve Him because I love Him? Where do I stand and what lessons can I learn from the second commandment?

Exodus 20:1–21 (continued)

Wholehearted for God

God's people are called to honour Him not just with their words but with their lives.

The third command taught the Israelites that they were to serve the Lord wholeheartedly (v.7). We tend to think that misuse of the name of the Lord meant blasphemy. It certainly did include this. However, it also included any use of the Lord's name which lacked sincerity. It is easy for us to take God's name on our lips without thought and to serve the Lord with our lips but not our hearts and lives. It is this fault, to which we are all prone, that the third commandment was especially directed.

Before we leave the third commandment we ought to add a few comments about the language in verses 5 and 6. There are many similar phrases in the Old Testament and it is clear that they are not to be understood literally. Rather the language is intended to emphasise the hatred God has of sin and the greatness of His blessing to those who follow Him in obedience. It is worth noting, however, that the results of sin almost inevitably extend to other people and generations than our own. Others suffer because we have sinned.

The fourth commandment was concerned with the observance of the Sabbath, which is explained in verses 8–11. One day in seven was required to be kept free from work in service to the Lord. There would appear to have been three reasons for this. Firstly, the enjoyment of God was intended to look back to the uninhibited fellowship which Adam and Eve had enjoyed with the Lord in the Garden of Eden. Then it was intended also to look forward to the time when God would fully deal with sin and enable His people to enjoy again unfettered communion with Him. Thirdly, it was intended to remind the people of the right of God over their lives: to all their time, money and energies. Thus, it was a reminder that He expected lives devoted to Him.

The New Testament teaches us that Jesus was the final 'sabbath rest' of God. He was and is the one in whom we now enjoy full fellowship with God. He is the 'lord of the sabbath', the one who gives us rest (Heb 4; Matt 12:8; 11:28). Thus, the sabbath has been abolished (Gal 3:24–25; Col 2:16) and the celebration of special days has become a matter of individual conscience (Rom 14:5). However, the New Testament never fails to remind us that we are to become slaves of Jesus, devoted to Him and using all our time, talents and energy in His service. We do not fulfil the demands of the fourth commandment until this is true of us.

Questions

1. *We are to serve God not with our lips alone but with all of our lives. Are our lives consistent with the things we say or sing? Are we near to breaking the third commandment?*

2. *God wants all of our lives and not just a part. In what areas of my life am I in danger of holding back from God what is due to Him? Am I willing to allow Him to do with my life whatever He wants?*

Oaths

The third commandment, and Jesus' words in Matthew 5:33–37 have been understood as forbidding Christians from ever taking oaths. This is a mistake. The Old Testament permitted and even required oaths in certain circumstances. Holy men and women are described as taking oaths (Gen 14:22–24; 21:23,24; 24:3,9; 26:31;
28:20,22; 31:53; 47:31; 50:5; Josh 9:15; Judg 21:5; Ruth 1:16–18; 2 Sam 15:21; 1 Kings 18:10; 2 Chron 15:14,15 etc.). God Himself is recorded as swearing in the Bible (Ps 132:11; Gen 22:16; 26:3; Ps 89:3,49; 110:4; Jer 11:5; Luke 1:73). Jesus also submitted to an oath (Matt 26:63,64), as did Paul (2 Cor 1:23; Gal 1:20). What the Bible does teach is that oaths are

to be regulated. We should never make an oath to 'talk big' and, probably, should never use them in ordinary conversation. However, when they are entered into they should be taken with all seriousness. When we make an oath we are going before the court of heaven and before the judge of all the world!

Exodus 20:1–21 (continued)

Caring for life and society

The Israelites were called by God to show an unselfish concern for others. In the same way we are expected to show a loving, caring and practical attitude toward others.

We have already noticed that these laws were intended to teach that wholehearted obedience to God was to include a God-centred lifestyle displayed in concern for others. It is this emphasis that is especially made in the last six commandments.

Of fundamental importance to God was that His people respected His institutions for society. At the heart of His purpose for mankind lay a properly ordered family life (see Gen 2:24). Thus, the preservation of good family life and of the marriage which was the heart of the family was legislated for in the fifth and seventh commandments. First, mutual respect and love was demanded and is no less required in the New Testament (Eph 6:1–4). No successful family can ever be built unless there is a mutual giving and sharing among its members. Though the commandment only required the respect of children it expected that that respect be deserved. The same remains true today. And a society which places great emphasis on good families continues to have the proper foundation for its own well-being.

The sixth commandment was intended to encourage respect for life (v.13). Properly understood, it would not only have been seen as banning murder. It would also have been recognised that it commanded men and women to do everything to improve the life of one another. Jesus certainly understood this command thus (Matt 5:21–26) and, no doubt, the godly in ancient Israel would have seen this too. There are so many ways in which we can spoil the lives of others. We can say hurtful things and either do, or fail to do, things which prevent others from enjoying the life which God has given them to the full. Whenever we do this we show that our obedience to the Lord is incomplete and we grieve Him.

The seventh commandment is found in verse 14. It prohibited adultery. The reason for this was probably twofold. On the one hand, it was God's purpose that sexual relationships were a symbol of lives devoted to one another in marriage. Secondly, and practically, adultery attacked the fabric of society in undermining family life (see above). Despite the wholesale rejection of the standards set out in the Bible by large groups of men and women today the wisdom of God's word is evident. Where family life is attacked and where sexual sin is permitted or even encouraged the social fabric breaks down. This is the testimony of the Bible, of history and the present day. Sadly, the lesson is so often ignored, even by professing Christians who like to think they know better than God.

Jesus taught that this, and the other commands, were not intended merely to govern our conduct but also our thoughts (Matt 5:27–30). This is very wise. It is the person who thinks right who will do the right things. The reason that so many Christians disobey clear instructions from God is surely because they have not learnt to think like Him. But Paul calls us to be renewed in the way we think (Rom 12:1,2) so that we may recognise the right course of action, welcome it and do it.

Questions

1. As we reflect upon the way in which society is organised around us, to what extent does God's will be seen to be disregarded? In what way does this particular passage challenge specific issues in our own society today, and what can we do about it?

2. Christians are called to care for life and society. As we consider the principles set out in these verses, how might we seek to live for God and encourage His standards to be observed more fully? Are there people or groups to whom we fail to show the care and respect that God expects of us? What might we do to put this right?

3. Christians are called to 'think straight'. Do I allow myself to be moulded in my thinking by the word of God or the world around me? Could my struggles and failures in some areas of my life be the result of failing to know and be convinced of God's way? What might I do to help myself think God's thoughts after Him?

Capital Punishment

Christians have sometimes believed that the sixth commandment forbids capital punishment and teaches that they should not go to war (see 'The Christian and War'). It is doubtful that the Bible teaches this. In Genesis 9:4–6 God taught Noah that life was sacred and that offences against a person's life should be treated very seriously indeed. This belief lies behind many of the laws in the Old Testament. The Old Testament writers believed that a person who acted against God in taking another person's life must be made aware of the seriousness of the offence. In fact, they taught that such a person forfeited his or her right to life. Executioners were sometimes appointed to act on God's behalf in order to effect the death penalty.

Today, we should regard all offences against sacredness of life very seriously. We should seek to encourage our governments to do the same. However, the detailed application of God's word will vary. Mercy is not out of place, especially where evidence of repentance is found. Thus, David the murderer was forgiven by God and he died peacefully.

The Christian and War

The Old Testament permitted war and the New Testament teaches that all of God's people have an obligation to their rulers (1 Sam 15:1; Rom 13:1–7; 1 Pet 2:13–16). Most Christians believe that it is sometimes necessary for a state, in a sinful world, to go to war. The Christian has a responsibility to the state and this includes sometimes using weapons against other men and women. It is not this sort of killing that is forbidden here. Murder is where one man deliberately kills another man out of hatred for him. In war few people enjoy killing others or wish to do so.

Exodus 20:1–21 (concluded)

Selfless attitudes

God expects His people to show both love and an awed respect for Him and to show this in practical ways as they live among others.

The eighth commandment (v.15) was intended to encourage the Israelites to respect one another's property. In its widest application it would have been seen as a demand for prompt and fair payment, the proper use of the things that God had given for the benefit of others, the wise use of God-given resources as well as forbidding theft. The Israelites were called to be good stewards of all that God had given them and to be devoted to the care and welfare of others, even above themselves. This is no less the responsibility of Christians today. Selfishness lies at the heart of most sins and most of the actions which disturb the harmony of God's people. But selfishness is hated by the Lord.

This honour for others is seen especially in the last two of the Ten Commandments (vv.16,17). The first forbade all false statements and comments made about others: as well as rebuking lies in a law court. How often we gossip, spread malicious half-truths or untruths about others. How little we respect the other person's integrity. And how destructive is such action. But we are called to reflect upon the good in others (Phil 4:8,9). What a difference there would be in the world and in church life if we honoured the Lord's command!

The last commandment condemned coveting (v.17). God listed those things which were most highly treasured in the society of ancient Israel. He did not condemn people for wanting these things. However, the Lord did condemn jealousy of those who had things that another did not have. He rebuked the selfish attitude which wanted these things at the expense of others. It is this attitude which continues to lie at the heart of many, if not most, ambitions. But it is selfish and hated by the Lord.

It is not His desire that we should want things just for ourselves. The Israelites had freely received from the Lord more blessings than they could possibly have hoped for. The example of the Lord was to be copied by them. Jesus' words 'freely you have received, freely give' (Matt 10:8) capture the spirit that was expected of the ancient Israelites and is similarly expected of us.

Clearly this commandment dug deeper than the five which preceded it. Paul realised this (Rom 7:7–12). It was intended to judge not the actions of men but their attitudes. In this way it emphasised how the earlier laws were to be understood. Jesus did nothing new in emphasising the importance of the heart in Matthew 5: the original law had made plain that God was as concerned for attitudes as actions.

At this point the Lord's charter for ancient Israel came to an end. And yet it concluded in such a way as to teach the people that they were constantly in need of grace. What the Lord required of them was such as to place them for ever as debtors to Him. Such a code of law, properly understood, could never encourage anyone to think that they could achieve what God required of them. However, the Ten Commandments would have also stood as a measure of a truly believing life. Only those who found their attitudes increasingly match those of the Lord could be confident that they really were the children of God. Equally, those tempted to think that their actions were upright would be persuaded that they were helpless to achieve the righteousness that God demanded of His friends.

This remains true today. As we reflect upon the righteousness of God displayed in these verses we can do no other than join the tax collector who said, 'Lord, be merciful to me a sinner' (Luke 18:13). This is true even if we are Christians. Though we have experienced the renewal of our minds and begin to approve the things that God loves, we are still far from perfect obedience. Until we die we can do no more than rejoice in the mercy of God. Above all, we have the privilege of knowing the one to whom the Ten Commandments pointed. There is one, the Lord Jesus, who perfectly fulfilled all God's righteous demands and through whom we receive the grace of God by faith. Hallelujah!

Verses 18–21 conclude this section of Exodus by describing the way the Lord accompanied His commands with His presence. Appropriately, He revealed Himself in a way which was intended to arouse awe and reverence of Him (v.20). In this way the people would be encouraged in the path of obedience, fearful of disobeying Him.

Thus two motives for obedience of the Lord are given in chapter 20: His love and His awesome majesty (vv.2,20). The Christian religion has always been in danger of emphasising one or other of these attributes of God at the expense of the other. Different Christian traditions often reflect this fact. We need to remember that the loving Jesus who is our saviour is also the majestic king of kings (see, especially, Rev 1:9–18).

Questions

1. What principles might we find in this passage which suggest that the unbelieving world is failing to honour God?

2. God expects us to be committed to unselfish attitudes and actions in all our dealings with one another. In what way do we allow selfish thoughts to enter our minds and lead to selfish actions? What can we learn from this passage as to why God expects us to live unselfishly? How can we put God's words into practice?

3. The Lord is a God of holy love. Do I believe this? What beliefs and actions might suggest that I do not take His love for me seriously enough? Are there things I say and do which suggest that I do give God's holiness a proper place in my life?

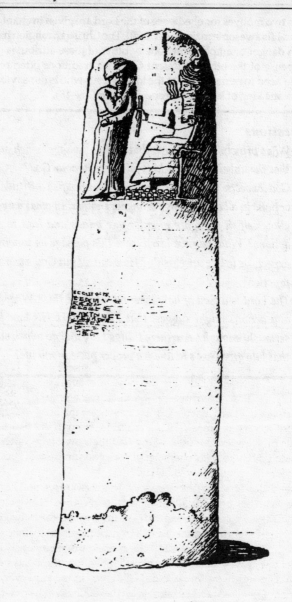

Fig. 2 An ancient law code

Exodus 20:22–26

God expects His people's worship to conform to His will

God here instructs His people that the way that they think about Him and offer Him worship is to be guided by what He says and not what they like or think.

The Ten Commandments set before us what proved to be timeless and fundamental moral principles. They came from God Himself (20:1). In this way the Israelites' morality (and ours, too) was based upon the will and character of the Lord, not on the opinions of the majority or those who held power. This was unique among the nations of the ancient world. Many had their own law codes. But none grounded the laws in the character of their gods or claimed specific divine origin for them in the way Israel did.

In the following chapters more specific laws were given. These laws did not cover every possible situation that might arise. However, they did suggest ways and provide examples of the way in which the great moral principles undergirding the Ten Commandments and other God-given principles were to be applied to the specific problems of society in the ancient world in which the Israelites lived. Often these laws have close parallels in other ancient law codes known to us. However, there are always differences and they emphasise the distinctive character of Israel's morality.

We are not called upon to insist on the detailed observance of these laws either in our societies or our churches. However, we are also not expected to ignore these chapters as so many Christians do. Rather we are expected to work out the demands of God for us in equally specific ways in our own differing situations. This is not always easy. Israel was both a state and the congregation of the people of God. From New Testament times this has never been true of any group of people (though sometimes men and women have acted as though it were true of them). The church and the state have different responsibilities. No nation can any longer think of itself as God's people. No church can claim an authority over the state, although the churches may wish to advise the state of its God-given responsibilities.

In the light of further truths that God has revealed, above all through Jesus, some of the practices and attitudes permitted in Old Testament times are forbidden to us.

Nevertheless, careful study of these chapters is of great value in encouraging faithful and practical discipleship. In addition to this these chapters also reveal those principles which God wishes to see honoured in society. As we reflect upon the teaching we need to be asking ourselves, 'How can this principle be applied to society today, though my society is (often) so different from that of Bible times?' (See 'Christians and the Law'.)

The specific laws begin and end with religious regulations (20:22–26; 23:14–19). This was surely significant and was intended to remind Israel that both the religious and social life of the people was to be governed by His revelation. It is popular for Christians to deny that the Scriptures are intended to regulate church life. Many practices have been adopted by Christian congregations without any thought as to what God has ordered. Often, it is suggested, the Scripture is the rule for faith and life but not the structure and activities of the church. No such distinction was found in the Old Testament and there is no suggestion that the New Testament believers accepted it.

Verses 22–23 repeated the earlier prohibition on images (20:4–6): a repetition which proved necessary in the light of the subsequent events with the golden calf (chapter 32). The Lord's repetitions are seldom given without good reason! We do well to give special attention to them.

The prohibition probably had reference to gods other than the Lord. However, it is true that Israel was never allowed to make an image of God. The reason for this is given in verse 22. The people's experience of the Lord (verses 18–21) had showed that the Lord could never be compared with images of gold and silver. A double danger would have arisen if an image had been made. It would have encouraged the people to have their thoughts of God limited by the image. It would also (see 20:4–6) have fostered the belief that the Lord could be manipulated.

In certain parts of the world any representation of God would encourage the belief that God can be manipulated, even today. And, while it is doubtful that pictures representing the Lord or Jesus are forbidden by this law it does suggest that we are to be very watchful that we do not confuse others or allow our conception of God and, especially, Jesus to be limited by any of the pictures we make. Equally, we must not allow our understanding of God to be clouded by the beliefs and opinions of unbelievers.

Verses 24–26 contain instructions about the altar. The altar was a central feature of Israelite religion and the two most important sacrifices are mentioned here. The burnt offering was like the passover: it turned aside God's wrath against the sinner by the provision of a substitute (see Lev 1). The fellowship offering declared the Lord's friendship with His people (Lev 3).

Significantly, both the altars described here were temporary structures. They were 'wanderer's altars' just as that described in 27:1–8. Unlike the nations around them the people of God were not expected to have sacred sites. Even Sinai never became a place of pilgrimage and worship. Rather, God was where His people were: always ready to forgive and provide fellowship. Eventually a Temple was built. But even then the first worshippers were unable to leave the opening celebrations without the king's words echoing in their ears, 'The heavens, even the highest heavens cannot contain you. How much less this temple that I have built' (2 Chron 6:18).

For the Christian believer it remains true that wherever the Lord leads us He is with us: ever ready to forgive us and share fellowship with us through the Lord Jesus. Thus, no church building can ever be a sacred place or sanctuary. God is with His people wherever they are.

The emphasis upon decency found in verse 26 was especially important in the ancient world where much religion was based around nakedness and sexual orgies (a fault which the Israelites fell into in chapter 32). No aspect of the worship of God was to so much as suggest that any comparison could be made between the religion of the Lord and pagan worship. Paul made the same point when writing to the Corinthians (1 Cor 14:40). Since Corinth was well known for its corruption and evil practices it is likely that a concern for purity lay behind his words. It is easy for Christians to be naive about this. I have been at worship with other believers when sensual dress and actions have been an unhelpful distraction.

Questions

1. *The lives of our churches are to be governed by the will and word of God. When we decide what to do in our church and we say what we think, are we directed by what God says or what we want? What issues are before our church at the moment? How might the lessons of this section be applied to the present situation?*

2. *It is almost impossible not to have some picture of God in our mind. But is the picture I have one which is in danger of denying some of the great and wonderful things that God has revealed about Himself? Can I think of ways that I might try to avoid falling into this danger?*

Christians and the Law

Over the centuries Christian believers have differed in the way they have believed the laws of the Old Testament apply in their time.

Some deny that the law has any continuing value today. We now live in the time of the Spirit and He it is who leads us to do the things that please God; we do not need anything else.

Some argue that the law continues to be valid today; all of it. They say that God does not change and neither do the laws by which He righteously governs the world. Thus, the laws remain standards which He would like to see fulfilled today.

Most Christians tend to be a bit selective! They suggest that the Ten Commandments have a continuing value and force but most of the other laws are either fulfilled in the work of Jesus on the cross (the sacrificial laws, for example) or were temporary rules given to the state of Israel.

Increasingly, a fourth view is being adopted. The view (assumed here) says several things. Firstly, it recognises that all of the laws have a continuing value since they reflect the moral character of the unchanging God. Secondly, it recognises that we live in a very different world! This has two consequences. We live the other side of the events associated with Jesus' first coming. He it is who shows us how these laws are to be lived and in whom many are, truly, fulfilled. The other consequence is that we need to discover what were the principles that governed the advice given to Israel and how those same principles apply in our very different world.

Exodus 21:1–11

People are more important than things

God expects His people to be more concerned for people than 'things' and to show compassion, care and justice to those who are in especial danger of being ignored or exploited.

Neither the Old nor the New Testaments try to set up political, social or economic systems which are especially approved of by God. The reason for this is that the Scriptures realise that the problems of injustice and unfairness are seldom simply the result of the system but arise from the existence of sinners who pervert the system.
While there are certainly some evil systems the difficulty is as often with the fact that there is no shortage of sinners ready to pervert any system to their own advantage and not use it to the benefit of all.

Thus, rather than attack the social and economic system which was found in all the surrounding nations in the ancient world, the Lord sought to make laws which would encourage the proper attitude between people and ensure fairness and justice.

This is illustrated in the first section of social laws which God revealed to Israel. Chapter 21 is devoted to a discussion of personal rights before property rights are considered in chapters 22 and 23. This, itself, is important. People, not things, are more important to God and offences against people were to be more severely punished.

Still more interesting is the fact that God turns first to the rights of slaves.

In ancient society slaves were considered the property of their owner with few, if any, rights of their own. But it is this group of people, who were most likely to suffer injustice, who were first legislated for by the Lord.

Two different slavery practices were legislated for (21:1–11). First (vv.1–6), consideration was given to the man who had voluntarily offered himself as a slave. Then (vv.7–11) attention was given to the woman who had been sold as a slave-wife. Significantly, the most usual way (both then and now) to obtain slaves – by kidnapping – was forbidden to the Israelites (v.16). Slavery by force or conquest was, therefore, made impossible.

Having removed the greatest abuse of the slavery system the Lord proceeded to regulate the remaining practices. Verses 2–6 provided regulations which set out the terms under which a man or woman were to become slaves. That women slaves were to have the same rights is clearly taught in Deuteronomy 15:12. When a man or woman voluntarily offered themselves for service the following conditions were to apply. The person was to be released in the same marital condition in which he or she entered service (v.3). However, if the master had given a man a slave-wife (see vv.7–11) two rights appeared to be in conflict and legislation was required. On the one hand the man had a right to his freedom. But the master had a right to the woman whom he had purchased as a slave-wife. The former slave was, therefore, not to take advantage of his master's generous provision of a wife. The first right was to have priority over the second. A compassionate alternative was, however, provided (vv.5,6) which maintained the rights of both parties. Doubtless, few men would have been willing to marry a slave-wife without intending such a course of action. Interestingly, Deuteronomy 15:13,14 captured the compassionate nature of God's laws when it taught that the departing slave was to leave with as much as he could carry away with him. He was to be given a second chance to make a success of his life and was given every encouragement not to fail! Since many men would have been forced into slavery as a result of their own folly this is a quite remarkable provision of a merciful God!

Verses 7–11 describe a different situation. It describes a woman who has been sold into slavery as a slave-wife. This was a popular means of avoiding the payment of a dowry. In many parts of the world today the dowry is still found. It is a payment made by the bride's family to the husband's family intended to enable them to assume responsibility for the woman without incurring loss. However, a poor family in ancient Israel might have been unable to raise a dowry. This would have meant that the daughter would either have to remain unmarried or be sold as a slave-wife. This arrangement would have benefited both parties. A bride price would not have had to be paid for the woman and a dowry would have been unnecessary. A woman purchased according to this system was, therefore, purchased for life. This explains why the normal law of release did not apply (v.7). However, if the slave owner went back on his previous intention she still had rights. She could be purchased back by her own family (v.8). Moreover, unless she was given the rights of a full member of the slave owner's family and the rights of a wife (vv.9,10) she had complete freedom to leave (v.11). The law was, thus, given to protect the woman and give her her rights. Practical compassion for a person most likely to suffer cruelty was provided by this law. At the same time the rights of the owner were preserved.

There is a huge difference between these two laws and those of the surrounding societies in the ancient world. Other societies regarded slaves as 'things' with no rights. God's law established slaves as persons with the full rights to justice that all other people were to have.

In the modern world there are many men and women whose basic rights to fairness and justice are ignored. Christians have always been ready to join hands with others in order to right such wrongs. We are called to speak out on such matters. However, it is not just in our world that these truths are ignored. Too often the Church fails to remember that all men stand before God as equal. In Christ, 'there is neither Jew nor Greek, slave nor free, male nor female' (Gal 3:28). Yet how often have James' words about favouritism applied to Christians and churches (Jas 2:1–12).

Questions

1. God wants to see fairness and justice upheld and dispensed with mercy. In what way do the principles of this passage apply to the way we treat other people and what sort of things in our own society and world must grieve God (and ought to grieve us)? What can we do about it?

2. In what ways may our church fail to put into practice the teaching of this section of God's word?

3. God considers people more important than things. Is this true of my attitudes and actions? In what areas of my life do I put things above the needs of those around me?

Exodus 21:12–36

Encounter and response

This passage taught the Israelites (as it teaches us!) that if a person had really met with God then their lives would be different and that the difference would be seen, above all, in his or her lifestyle.

We have seen that the Bible regards life as sacred and teaches that offences against a person's life were to be treated very seriously by the Israelites. This same principle was again stated in 21:12. However, it was then followed by a quite remarkable law. God made a distinction between deliberate and accidental killing (vv.13,14).

In many parts of the world, even today, a death leads to a blood-feud between families or groups of people. In such circumstances little thought seems to be given as to whether the killing was accidental. Death must be avenged by another death. This sort of attitude was forbidden among the Israelites. The accidental manslayer was to be given protection. But deliberate murder was to be punished. Jesus understood that these laws also applied to the general attitudes of men to one another and to actions which hinder the enjoyment of life of someone else (Matt 5:21–26). We need to be sure that we are obedient to Him.

Some of these laws given to Israel seem strangely harsh. This is especially true of verses 15 and 17. Verse 15 almost certainly demands the death penalty for someone striking his or her parent. Verse 17 calls for the same punishment for swearing at them! These laws were harsh even in a harsh world! However, to understand these laws we have to remember that Israel were the people of God. As such they were expected to show attitudes far different from the surrounding pagan nations. God had already revealed to them His high respect for the family (20:12). In their family lives the Israelites were to show what a difference it made to be the children of God. However, if they conducted themselves no differently from the unbelieving people who were around them, they failed in their testimony (see again Gen 12:1–3) and by living in such a way showed that they were really strangers to the grace of God. As the people of God, Israel was to show that such people stood under the judgment and wrath of God. They were no longer part of the people of God and must suffer the punishment for sin.

The Bible never tires of emphasising that true believers will show in all their relationships that they have experienced God's grace. Those who fall should be regarded as unbelievers. Churches should not tolerate as members those whose lives deny the Gospel.

Verses 18–27 deal with the penalties that are to follow personal injuries. The fundamental principle which is to govern the assessment of compensation is set out in verse 23. This law has often been understood as demanding exact retribution and has been criticised as a result. In fact it was a remarkable law for its time since it was intended to ensure that any penalty should not exceed the damage done. There is always a tendency for men to over-react to the hurts others have inflicted on them (see Gen 4:23–4 for a good example). This is forbidden here. Equally, the law teaches that the injured person must not suffer as a result of the injury. Loss of earnings had to be fully compensated (vv.18–19), excessive punishment of a slave was forbidden (vv.20–1), miscarriage brought on as a result of a blow required compensation (v.22) and a severely injured slave gained his freedom (vv.26–7). Again the concern for slaves is very prominent in these laws (see above).

The principles here are the foundation for justice in any society. But they must not lead to the attitude which marked Jews at the time of Jesus (Matt 5:38–48). A concern for just retribution had become a revengeful spirit in Jesus' day. But He called for a very different attitude: a compassion even for enemies and a willingness to suffer wrong rather than demand one's rights. See 'Jesus' teaching on the Law'.

The next paragraph (21:28–36) follows naturally from the last section of the law. How is a man or woman liable to the injured person (or animal) when their own animals have caused the hurt? The section deals with the harm an ox, the most usual domestic animal to cause injury, might do to humans (vv.28–32) or other animals (vv.35–36). It also discusses the liability of the owner of a pit into which an animal falls (vv.33–34).

Several important principles are set out. No one is to be liable for a complete accident (v.28). However, to safeguard others from danger the animal must be slaughtered (v.28). To implant the horror of murder the meat was not to be eaten. Accidents do not always prove to be accidental. Often they are the result of negligence. Where negligence is proved the animal's owner was to be regarded as a murderer and punished accordingly (v.29). This may seem harsh but would have had a powerful effect upon the people and would have encouraged them to do all that they could to protect their fellow-citizens from danger and harm. Moreover, a distinction was made between negligence leading to loss of life and murder (v.30). A murdered life could not be compensated for by monetary payment. Death as the result of goring by an ox could however be met by the payment of compensation. These laws were to apply even to children and servants (vv.31,32) and adequate compensation paid. This was emphasised by the fact that the full price of a slave had to be repaid (v.32).

Negligence leading to the death of an animal was also to be met by the payment of compensation (vv.33–34,36).

Yet it is the law in verse 35 that captures the spirit of this section of the law best of all. When one animal accidentally killed another the burden of the loss was to fall equally upon both the owners. In this way the care and concern for one's neighbour required by the Lord was perfectly illustrated. We might think, 'Why should the person who has done nothing wrong suffer?'. The Bible responds, 'Why should the person who has suffered loss not find help and support from his neighbour, even when the cost is high (for a bull was a valuable item in an ancient household)?'

It is this spirit which God Himself has shown to us and which He expects of us. He sent His Son into this world. At great cost that Son suffered and died for the needs of others. We are called to show the same attitude to one another (Phil 2:5–11).

Questions

1. *A person who has encountered God can never be the same again. Once again, as we face this challenge, what evidence can we (and those around us) see which testifies to the reality of our experience of God? What areas of our lives have we neglected or not allowed God's Spirit to enter and change?*

2. *A true believer will willingly suffer to serve God. Do I show the marks of spiritual maturity by being willing to do anything for the sake of others or do I insist on my own way and my rights? What steps do I need to take to put this right?*

Exodus 22:1–17

Fairness and friendship

God expects His people to show restraint when attacked by others and to be always motivated by a desire to heal broken and strained relationships.

Chapter 22:1–17 is a section concerned with legislation for the protection of property. In modern society there is an increasing tendency to punish theft more severely than murder. Though the penalties for theft were great in ancient Israel they were far less than the penalties for murder. This shows the Bible's attitude. Indeed verses 2–3 emphasise this in a most vivid way. A burglary at night may lead to the death of the thief. In the dark the culprit cannot be recognised and self defence against someone who may have a dangerous weapon is understandable. However, in the daytime the situation is different. Usually, it is far more easy to assess the situation and danger. We may presume that the law here assumes that there is no danger. In such circumstances the man who has been burgled is not to take the law into his own hands and certainly must not inflict a punishment out of all proportion to the crime (see 21:14). Even the thief has a right to life. If he is murdered his assailant is to be fully punished.

The remaining verses in this section deal with: the theft of an animal (vv.1–4); damage to property caused by negligence (vv.5–6); the loss of goods while under the protection of another (vv.7–15) and the loss incurred through the seduction of a daughter (vv.16–17).

The thief who was caught in ancient Israel had to pay compensation for

131

the theft as well as payment made by way of punishment. The extent of the punishment doubtless would have discouraged theft and emphasised why such actions were hated by the Lord (20:15). The penalty reflected the value of an ox, in particular, and the many years sometimes required to train the animal.

The laws for negligence are similar in principle, to those in 21:29,33–34,36. Those which deal with the loss of property in the possession of another are fairly clear and obviously sensible. They ensure the resolution of what could be a most embarrassing situation and seek to minimise the likelihood of ill-will developing. The laws in the Old Testament were never simply concerned with what was right. They also sought to heal broken or strained relationships. This was vital in a society where people could not avoid meeting one another frequently. The New Testament shows a similar concern for the unity and harmony of the people of God. It was this, rather than the rights and wrongs of the matter that concerned the Apostle Paul when Euodia and Syntyche disagreed in Philippi (Phil 4:1–3). Yet how few churches show the same zeal for harmony.

Unlike some of the surrounding nations, women were not regarded as property in Israel. A dignified status was given them (see Prov 31:10–31). Nevertheless, if a virgin daughter was seduced it would lead to financial loss for her father since he would not be able to ask the usual bride-price for her. This explains why verses 16–17 are included at this point. Interestingly, here it is only the bride price that is required (even if the man does not choose to marry her). Probably, it is assumed that she acted as a willing party. Proven rape seems to have been more severely treated (Deut 22:25–28).

Questions

1. *What lessons can we learn from this passage about the principles that should guide those in authority in making decisions?*

2. *We are to be merciful and fair in all our dealings with others. Is it not true that we easily over-react to the hurts others inflict on us? As we consider this passage what should we learn and then seek to do when faced with hurts?*

3. *Peace-making is to characterise the true believer. What is the foremost motive that governs my relationships with others? Am I concerned for my rights or for peace and harmony? In what areas of my life do I need to apply the lessons taught here?*

Exodus 22:18–20

Trust and obey

God's people are taught the need to humbly trust God in all things and to live in obedience to His will for their lives.

The remainder of chapter 22 is divided into three sections:

1. Verses 18–20 describe fundamental perversions of God's purpose for mankind and His appointed punishments;
2. Verses 21–27 set out for Israel their responsibilities to underprivileged members of society;
3. Verses 28–31 state several responsibilities which His people had for the Lord Himself.

God created men and women to share His own character and personality and to enjoy unhindered His fellowship and the world He had designed for their pleasure. The full enjoyment of the world He had made depended on its proper use, for nothing misused works or functions as well as when it is used properly. Sin intervened. However, God called Abraham and his descendants and redeemed them so that they might, once again, reflect God's purpose and will for men and women. They were to set before all the nations of the world God's hatred of everything sinful and His judgment of wickedness and evil.

With this in mind we can understand these verses. There could be no place in Israel for those who refused to offer worship to the Lord alone (v.20). There was to be no place for people with divided loyalty (see 20:3).

The prohibition on sorcery and, presumably, all occult practices (see also Lev 20:27) had the same purpose. Whatever the reality lying behind the occult, it offered means of revealing the future and information which God had forbidden to men and women. Thus, it revealed a lack of faith in God and an unwillingness to trust Him and use the means He had appointed of finding His will. There could be no place for such faithless conduct among the people of God. The same is true today. And it is not the occult alone that we should avoid. All too often professing Christians seem incapable of living by faith.

Unless they are surrounded by props to their faith they seem to have no faith at all! What a world of difference there would be if believers actually learned to lean entirely upon the Lord and His promises.

God planned and ordered His world. For this reason He had given to men and women their sexual desires. Aroused by them they would find true fulfilment in life in the exclusive and complimentary relationship which God had planned for them (see Gen 2:20–24). To engage in sexual activity outside of this relationship was a denial of God's fundamental and good purpose for men and women. Such a disregard for Him (especially in the case mentioned in verse 19) was a clear declaration that the culprit knew nothing of God's grace and could not, therefore, be one of His people. Those who were not the Lord's children were under His judgment. The penalty in such circumstances was death. Such a sinner was no better than an Egyptian!

While it is right for Christians to seek to uphold the moral standards of the Lord, it is to the Church that these words most obviously apply today. The severity of God's judgment in such cases is intended to indicate that nobody who acts in a way which is opposed to God's revealed will has any right to call themselves a Christian. While there is forgiveness with God, and while we are all sometimes overwhelmed by sin, persistent rebellion against God's will shows that we have never really known Him. In the book of Revelation these very sins, among others, are used to emphasise that unforgiven actions of this sort will exclude a person from the kingdom of God (Rev 21:8).

Thus, Christian churches must discipline all those who engage in any form of conduct which denies the faith of the Lord Jesus. To fail in this is to create confusion. God must be seen to be holy and to require holiness of His people. We must not allow any to think that they are eternally secure when they may stand in danger of Hell fire. We must act for their own good (see 1 Cor 5:5 where Paul makes this very point).

Questions

1. There are things that God really hates. From this passage, what things in our own society does it appear that God must hate?

2. Christians are called to live by faith in the promises of God. Do we know God well enough to know what His will is? Do we have sufficient faith to believe Him or do we need other supports to convince us that He really loves us? How might we help our faith to grow?

3. All Christians are to obey God in everything. Is this true of me? What do these verses teach me about the importance and blessings of obedience?

Exodus 22:21–27

Compassion and care

God expects His people not only to hate sin but to love the good. Thus, they are called to show compassion and care especially to those who are in danger of exploitation and injustice.

All that God has just said must not let us think that the Lord only hates that sort of conduct that most moral people would also despise. Thus, in verses 21–27, God reveals His wish that His people are expected to show care and compassion to all, especially those in every society who are in greatest need. Any conduct by believers which fails at this point is equally hated by Him. Yet how little attention God's people give to the attitudes expected of them which are revealed in these verses!

The importance of these laws was immediately impressed upon the people by the reminder, 'you were aliens in Egypt' (v.21). The Lord had shown compassion to a poor, helpless people in Egypt. The same attitude was, therefore, required of them. No less is true of us. We were helpless in sin but God did everything He could, even to the death of His own Son, to show us mercy. It is extraordinary if we do not show mercy to those whose needs are as great as ours were!

The groups of people mentioned here were those who were most likely to be in need in ancient society. An alien (v.21) was a non-Israelite who was living with the people of God but who did not have full citizenship. They did not have family property which was handed down from generation to generation. Usually, they would have earned a living by day-labouring.

They may not have had access to the judicial system of Israel. Thus, they were in danger from fraud and exploitation and from being despised as members of another race. Widows and orphans were vulnerable (as in so many societies today) because they did not have an adult male to provide a living for them and protect their interests. A failure among the Israelites to show practical compassion for these people was a very serious matter. The Lord threatened death upon culprits – but did not delegate the responsibility to anyone else. He would act. Once again, we notice that the penalty is that which symbolised complete exclusion from the people of God. Just as the Egyptians became widows and orphans as a result of God's judgment, so the Israelites would suffer the same fate.

The New Testament is no less concerned for the Lord's people to show compassion and emphasises that the Gospel of Jesus breaks down the barriers between men which lead to the exploitation of one by the other (Eph 2:11–22). Love is to be shown, even for enemies (Matt 5:43–48, see 'Jesus and the Law'). We are not only to meet the needs of others but to lavish help upon them (Matt 5:38–42). This is the mark of a true disciple: a real Christian.

The law given in verses 25–27 has often been misunderstood. Many Christians have concluded that it forbids taking interest on loans. This misses the whole point of the original law. The purpose of the law was not to provide rules for the financing of business ventures. Presumably, in such circumstances Israelite law would have allowed loans. Rather this law was given by God to protect the poor in society who were forced to seek a loan because of their poverty. In many societies today the poor are crippled by the interest payment due on loans which they had to seek because of their desperate need. It is this danger that God's law seeks to avoid. Where a genuine need existed it was the religious duty of the Israelite to help. The Lord was compassionate and expected the same conduct of His people (v.27). Moreover, if a pledge was sought to guarantee the repayment of the loan, it was to be returned when needed (vv.26,27). Such open-handed generosity was expected of God's people. It characterised the Church in its early years (see, for example, Acts 2:44,45) but is so often missing today. Few churches today could be commended like that in Macedonia (2 Cor 8:1–5) and yet Paul clearly regarded their generosity as a mark of their love for the Lord Jesus (2 Cor 8:8,9).

Questions

1. *What groups in our world and our society suffer from injustice? How do you think God feels about it and what can we do about such injustice?*

2. *God lavishes His compassion and care on every true Christian. Do we realise what He has done and is still doing for us? What effect does, or ought, this fact have upon our lives?*

3. *God expects those who have received His compassionate care to show it to others. How can I show this to my family, friends, my work-mates? What ought I to do when faced with the needs of the poor and needy in my world...my town?*

Jesus and the Law

The frequent misunderstanding of the relationship between verse 24 and Jesus' words in Matthew 5 suggest that an extended treatment of Jesus' teaching there might be useful.

Matthew 5:38–42

These verses provide the fifth application of Jesus' teaching in 5:17–20. Once again, Jesus quotes words from the Jewish traditional interpretation of the Old Testament. He again finds it necessary to show how the Jews were wrong in understanding the Old Testament laws. The Jews had rightly summarised the teaching of Exodus 21:24; Leviticus 24:20 and Deuteronomy 19:21 in the words which Jesus quotes. Jesus shows, however, that the Jews had not properly understood these words. In the Old Testament the instructions given (see especially Deut 19:18) were for the magistrate. The laws were intended to provide principles upon which decisions in law should be taken. There were two reasons for this teaching. First, the law was intended to regulate revenge and retaliation. In addition, the law was intended to remove punishment from the realm of person vengeance to that of the law court. If a wrong had been committed then the only place for the wrong to be put right was in the court of law. The law was intended to provide justice. Indeed, the Jews realised this. On the basis of this law proper rules for compensation had been developed for personal injury.

However, in verse 39 Jesus makes it quite clear why He disagreed with the Jews' interpretation of these laws. The Jews had extended the principle of the law so that it became a guideline for personal conduct. In this way they reversed the original intention of the law. Jesus also taught that, as with the other laws, the words apply to individual motives. If we understand Jesus' words in this way we can see that Jesus is not speaking about national events. There is no possible reason to believe that on the basis of these words Jesus intended to teach either pacifism or non-resistance as a citizen of society. In Romans 13 and 1 Peter 2 the relationship of the individual to the structures of society are described. Jesus is not talking about these things. Consequently, Jesus is not teaching that a Christian should never go to law. Jesus is not teaching that a man should not resist intruders into his house. Jesus is not teaching that a person should recklessly dispense with his goods.

It is clear that Jesus is attacking the misunderstanding of the Old Testament law by the scribes and the Pharisees. Their misunderstanding was such that they interpreted these words of the Old Testament to encourage revenge and retaliation in which the person is repaid in exactly the same way as he has offended.

In verses 39–42 Jesus gives a number of examples of how a disciple should conduct himself before others. First, in verse 39 He describes the reaction of a true disciple to personal insult. The picture Jesus gives is not one of violent physical attack. However, He describes what was regarded as the greatest possible insult in Palestine. A slap on the cheek might hurt but it did not hurt so much as the insult it carried with it.

Jesus is, therefore, applying himself to the realm of personal insults, however serious. Jesus' words are not necessarily intended to be understood literally but are rather an attempt to illustrate how a Christian is not to meet an insult by another insult or revenge. In addition to this, Jesus seems to imply that a true disciple will have a loving and friendly spirit even towards those who bring the greatest insults. The disciple will always be loving and forgiving.

In verse 40 Jesus describes the disciples' reaction to those who try to take advantage. This appears to be the point of Jesus' illustration. Very often in the world we live in men try to take advantage over one another. Indeed, often the person who follows such a course is regarded as a clever person if he can do it well and get away with it. We hear much of personal rights today. But a disciple does not consider he has any rights at all and he is willing to suffer at the hands of others. We need to carefully understand Jesus' words. He is not speaking literally. It does not mean a man never reacts to those who take advantage of him. A man may for the sake of justice and the rights of others defend himself. But the disciple is called to keep pure. A disciple would happily endure if he were the only one to be affected.

Jesus then moves on to give two further illustrations which emphasise the attitudes which He is trying to encourage. In verse 41 Jesus describes the Christian's reaction to those duties which are placed upon him. The illustration that Jesus makes is of a levy of labour which was a legitimate practice in the land of Palestine and was a duty which a citizen must not refuse. It was not popular, rather like tax-paying is not popular today. Many found it extremely inconvenient. The Pharisees would have grudgingly obeyed. They would have done exactly what was required of them – no more. A man asked to walk a mile would measure every pace to make sure he did not do too much. This is not the standard of the disciple, says Jesus. Duties are to be performed cheerfully and generously. This is true even if such duties are to our personal disadvantage.

The last illustration which Jesus gives teaches how the disciple should react to need. Jesus is not telling disciples what they are to do when people who live by begging ask them for help. Jesus does, however, have in mind genuine cases of need. When the disciple is aware of a case of need he will do all that he can to meet that need.

Matthew 5:43–48

Jesus begins His final example of true righteousness and how to understand the Old Testament laws by quoting Leviticus 19:18, and the words that the scribes and the Pharisees had added to that passage: 'and hate your enemy'. Once again Jesus teaches that this interpretation overthrows the original meaning of the Bible passage. The Jews' interpretation made a sharp distinction between a neighbour or friend and an enemy. The original law was intended to teach that love must always win over vengeance. Jesus shows that the question asked by the scribes and Pharisees: 'Who is my neighbour' (Luke 10:36) was wrong. The neighbour is anyone in need.

What then did Jesus mean when He commanded all true disciples to 'love your enemies'? To understand Him we need to notice that the New Testament has several words for love. First, there is a word for love between members of a family. This word refers to a general affection between people. Second, there is a word for the love which exists between a man or a woman and their best or closest friends. Third, there is a word for passionate love. This word emphasises the sensual and sexual aspects of love between a man and a woman. But Jesus does not use any of these words here. He knew the natural disposition of men and women. He does not condemn them nor does He suggest that any of them should be extended to everybody. Jesus knew family love. He knew how we more naturally get on with some people more than others. He knew that some people become intimate friends.

However, Jesus used another word for love. The word emphasises a person's will. It speaks of good intentions and helpful concern. It is an attitude which means that whatever a person does, however he treats us, insults and hurts us, we will never let bitterness enter our hearts. A true disciple will always seek the other person's good. This is something only a true disciple can do. It is evidence of God's work in the disciple. It emphasises, again, that a disciple is made right by God before he can do what is right. A disciple must, however, live in such a way. It is the only evidence that we are God's children. Jesus emphasises this in the first part of verse 45.

Jesus gives several other reasons why a disciple must live in this way. First, He gives the example of God Himself (verse 45). While God does have a special family love for His children (see Gen 17:21; Ps 103:17,18; Ps 147:20; Matt 11:25; Luke 12:32; Rom 8:1,28-39) He also has a concern for all men (Gen 17:20; 39:5; Ps 36:6; John 3:16). God shows this by treating all men in the same way.

In verses 46 and 47 Jesus gives another reason why disciples must love everyone. He tells His hearers that God's laws are intended to make His disciples different from unbelievers. But if God's disciples only act according to the same standards that unbelievers adopt, then there is no difference between them and there is no evidence of true discipleship.

Verse 48 is intended to conclude all of Jesus' teaching in verses 21-48. Jesus seems to have in mind the Old Testament passages in Leviticus 19:2 and Deuteronomy 18:13. The scribes and the Pharisees had only understood these Scriptures as referring to outward actions and then only to those which the Scriptures specifically commanded.

Exodus 22:28–31

Generous devotion

God teaches His people, in this passage, that He expects them to honour Him in the way they use both the money and the goods that He entrusts to their care.

The last four verses in chapter 22 recount several of the people's responsibilities to the Lord. Both the Lord (see 20:7) and the ruler were to be respected. The New Testament is equally explicit (1 Cor 13:1). See further our discussion earlier. The linking of the ruler and the Lord in the same law was probably intended to emphasise that to act against a ruler is to act against God Himself. While this does not rule out the conscientious withholding of obedience for Christ's sake (Matt 22:21) when a rule infringes the Lord's rights, it does stress a solemn responsibility to be good citizens.

Verse 29 is not very clear. However, it was probably intended as a reminder that the people were to support the Lord's work without doing so grudgingly. The support of the Tabernacle and the priesthood would have required a considerable annual income from God's people. A system of tithes and offerings was instituted to meet this need (see, for example, Lev 27:30–33; Num 18:21). These offerings were compulsory: rather like income tax today.

The New Testament sets no compulsory standard for the giving of God's people. However, it does teach us that our giving is to be done more generously and cheerfully. It guarantees the Lord's blessing on those who do so (2 Cor 9:6–15). Is the spiritual poverty of so many Christians and churches the result of disobedience and a failure to live faithfully in their giving?

It is not surprising that the next law (vv.29b,30) reminded the Israelites of their responsibility to give to the Lord the firstborn males in their families, herds and flocks. In the case of their sons a redemption payment was to be made (Ex 34:19–20). The firstborn animals were, however, to be sacrificed. It is clear from the Bible that the firstborn in Israel were representative of the people as a whole. Just as the judgment of God upon the firstborn in Egypt was intended as a statement of His wrath against the whole nation so His demand for the consecration of the firstborn in Israel was intended to teach His people that they were all to be holy to the Lord. Their lives were to be devoted to Him.

Paul made the same point in Romans 12:1 when speaking of all Christians. 'Offer your bodies as living sacrifices, holy and pleasing to God', he said. Thus, all our lives and the best that we are, are to be devoted to Him. When we see this, we are able to understand that the tithe (v.29a) was also intended to symbolise the same point. Whatever the level of our giving, and that will vary as a result of our personal circumstances, our gifts are to be offered up as a token of lives completely dedicated to the Lord. No other giving is acceptable to God.

Later, elaborate dietary laws were given to the Israelites. These laws made hygienic sense for a people in ancient Palestine. However, their purpose was symbolic. The laws were intended to make a distinction between the sacred and the non-sacred. These laws seem to have been especially given to the priests to emphasise the holiness of their responsibilities and duties. This thinking lies behind verse 31, though the particular reason why an animal torn by beasts should not be eaten is not known. Nevertheless, the fact that all the people were intended to observe the law taught them that they were *all* to be holy (Lev 19:2). There was no suggestion that the priests were to have a different standard of holiness than the rest of the people. All were to be priests in respect of the holiness of their lives (see 19:6).

The same demand rests upon Christians. Yet how often do believers give the impression that there is one standard of holiness for their leaders and another, far lower, for themselves. How often Christians excuse their own sinful actions by thinking that the Bible's standard of holiness does not apply to ordinary people like themselves! This law in Exodus exposes such thinking as the sin it really is.

143

Questions

1. Our world is full of people, groups and societies caught in the debt-trap. How must God view this? What do we think that Christian believers and others should do about this?

2. God's people are called to be devoted to Him. Do we have double standards? Do we expect one standard for ourselves and another for Christian leaders? Do we recognise that the one standard God requires of everyone is total commitment to Him?

3. Devotion to God is to be seen in His people being generous 'to a fault'. Could it be said of me that I over-do my giving to God of my time, gifts, resources (it is possible!) or am I over concerned with my rights, that others 'do their bit'; am I first in line to volunteer to meet a need or am I rarely, if ever, in the line at all?

Exodus 23:1–13

Truth, justice and compassion

God shows Himself deeply concerned for truthfulness and fairness. He wants groups and individuals to honour Him by showing respect for these standards.

Before the final ritual laws were given to Israel with which this lawcode concluded (23:10–19) several final principles of conduct were revealed by the Lord (23:1–9). The first group (vv.1–3) gave more detail to the law in 20:16. Five prohibitions were given with respect to the conduct of witnesses in a court of law. False testimony was forbidden, as was conspiracy to tell lies (v.1). Witnesses were to resist the pressure to side with the majority or give a testimony which the majority wanted to hear (v.2). Personal prejudice, especially in favour of the poor, was forbidden (v.3).

These temptations are often difficult to resist today. And though we may not be called as witnesses in a court of law our whole lives are to be governed by the same principles. We are to be disciplined in our speech (Jas 3:1–12) and our example is to be the Lord Jesus (1 Peter 2:22). His life and His words were always full of grace and truth (John 1:14). They always brought life and reconciliation. We cannot set ourselves a lower standard than Him.

Verses 4–5 reminded the Israelites that they were to show caring compassion, even for an enemy. The Lord Jesus taught the same truth (Matt 5:43–48, see 'Jesus and the Law') and in His own concern for the needs of sinners showed the standard which is to be copied by us.

145

The final verses of this section (vv.6–9) record the rules God gave to judges. They were to avoid bias (v.6) and were to examine the evidence carefully so as to avoid conviction on false charges (v.7). They were to assume the best about a person unless the evidence was conclusive against them (v.7b). They were not to be influenced by anything other than the truth (vv.8,9).

These words form the basis of all true justice. However, they do not just apply to judges. All too often, Christians are ready to share gossip and to condemn others on the basis of it without any serious attempt to arrive at the truth. Not infrequently, prejudice makes a believer automatically think the worst of some people. Too often people are not treated as individuals but are condemned because they are members of a certain group and are judged without evidence. If unbelievers act in such a way it is no excuse for believers who copy them. God forbids such conduct. He calls us to peace.

The laws ended, as they had begun, with laws given to regulate the religious life of the people (23:10–19). This was significant for it emphasised the Lord's sovereignty over all that the people did. These laws can be divided into two groups. The first provided legislation for the sabbath (vv.10–13) and the second was especially devoted to laws for the three annual festivals of Israel (vv.14–19).

The sabbath day had already been mentioned by the Lord (20:8). Here the principle of a sabbath day was extended to sabbath years (vv.10–11) which would have had the same symbolic purpose as the day. However, a new reason for the sabbath legislation was added by the Lord: the laws were intended to ensure that the poor in society should not starve (v.11) and that the whole of life be subject to a cycle of work and relaxation (vv.11,12).

These principles are no less applicable today. They remind us to pattern our lives in a proper way and remind governments of their responsibility to ensure that employees are not exploited by their employers in such a way as to deny them a proper rhythm of life.

Once again it is notable that the Lord showed such concern for those in danger of being exploited. We should not miss this emphasis in the law and should once again consider the application to our own lives.

Questions

1. *In what areas of our world can we see truthfulness and community care denied? How should we counter such threats to God's standards for us?*

2. *True believers are to be very careful how they use their tongues. In the light of this passage and the discussion above, what areas of our lives are characterised by a wrong use of our tongues? What practical steps might we take to avoid our abuses of speech?*

3. *Christians are to be fair and compassionate in all their conduct. As I review my conduct at home, at school or work, in my casual involvement with others, what improvements may I make to my own life and the care I show for others?*

Exodus 23: 14–33

Honouring the providing God

God's sheer generosity to His people demands their devoted obedience to Him and their total allegiance to Him, alone.

Verses 14–17 introduce the three great religious festivals of ancient Israel. We have already met the Feast of Unleavened Bread or the passover. The other two feasts reflected the farming background of the land to which God was leading His people.

The feast of the Harvest marked the end of the wheat harvest in June. Elsewhere it is called the Feast of Weeks. The feast of Ingathering also was known as the Feast of Booths or Tabernacles. It marked the end of the grape and olive harvest in the autumn. Indeed the passover seemed to mark the beginning of the barley harvest. All these feasts seemed to have a religious significance. Certainly, the first two commemorated the passover and the wilderness wanderings and the last became a festival for the celebration of the giving of the Law.

However, it is the agricultural importance of the feasts that had prominence in the laws given in these verses. The laws were intended to remind the people that it was the Lord who was the provider of all that they had been given. Since the gods of Canaan claimed to give fertility this repeated reminder was most essential. It is appropriate for Christians today to remind themselves that the Lord is the source of all that they have. And if we do not have the gods of Canaan we can easily forget His goodness to us, especially when we live in countries where all that we need is always available at the nearest shop.

The detailed regulations in verses 18–19 may seem rather obscure to us. However, leaven appears to have been a symbol of evil (Matt 16:6). This would have emphasised the need for perfect offerings to be made to the Lord. Thus the Israelites would have been reminded of the need for a perfect substitute to be offered in the place of their sin and their calling to be wholly dedicated to the Lord.

The law given in v.18b is understandable when we remember that a peace offering would normally be eaten on the same day it was offered (Lev 7:15). If the Lord's share was left to the next day it would have become uneatable. To offer uneatable food to the Lord would have been very disrespectful. We need to be very careful that we do not slip into doing things that are disrespectful to Him.

The law in verse 19a would have reminded the people that the Lord expected the best they were. It applies just as much to us today. The last law is explained by the fact that the Canaanites sacrificed a kid cooked in milk and the fields were then sprinkled with the dish to ensure their fertility. The people were to trust the Lord for their crops and not try to meet their needs faithlessly. Our lives are to be governed by our dependence on Him. We are not to do anything against God's will in order to try to get what we need.

Salvation by grace leads to obedience to the Lord. Obedience is the evidence that salvation has been truly received. It is the evidence of grace in the heart. Thus the list of the laws of ancient Israel concludes with a reminder that only obedience to God's demands in 20:1–23:19 would enable the people to enjoy the blessing of God upon His people (v.21).

The Lord promised that He would send His Angel to lead the people to victory (v.23). In the land they would enjoy the experience of life with the curse for sin removed (v.25). The language used at this point: the abolition of sickness and the guarantee of long life recalls the experience of Adam and Eve in the Garden before sin intervened. It also pointed forward to the final kingdom of God of which Canaan was only a shadow (Rev 21:3,4).

This explains why the Canaanites had to be wiped out from the land (vv.23,33) and their gods had to be removed (vv.29,30). There could be no place in His kingdom for either sin or sinners. As the sparing of Rahab was subsequently to show (Josh 6:17) the extermination of the Canaanites had a religious rather than a racial motivation. Rahab had accepted the God of Israel and was, therefore, able to claim full membership of His people.

Questions

1. *God expects His people to give Him honour. Considering the Scriptures we have just read, what areas of our lives are in danger of dishonouring God? What ought we to do about this?*

2. *God provides for the needs of His people. Do I believe this? Do I recognise His provision in the ordinary things of life, am I alert to His gifts when in special need, do I recognise His provision even when He does not give me what I want? How can I strengthen my faith by recognising His provision for me?*

Exodus 24:1–11

The family of God

God here reveals to His people the privileged status that they have both as His friends and members of His own family.

The first 23 chapters of Exodus may be very briefly summarised. God's people were freed to serve Him; they were delivered in order to respond to Him. He had taken the initiative to deliver them from bondage. He had redeemed them through the passover and had broken the power of Egypt at the Red Sea (chapters 1–5). The people had then been expected to respond to Him in an open commitment to the detailed will of God (chapters 19–23). Chapter 24:1–12 describes the relationship which the Lord then entered into with His people.

After we are told that the people were willing to obey the Lord (vv.3,4) a strange ceremony is described (vv.5–7). It would seem that what took place was a kinship ritual. Such rituals are still found in many parts of the world. In them, two people or groups pledge kinship to one another and accept the privileges and demands that such a relationship involves. Thus, the ceremony proclaimed to the people that they were the children of God: by grace in obedience. The Bible never fails to delight in this fact and emphasises over and over again God's pity and care for His children and the freedom with which He can be approached by them (Ps 103:13; Matt 18:13; 6:26,32; 7:9–11 etc.).

And yet the same ceremony also declared that the people were now pledged to the Lord. He had pledged His all to them. They must pledge their all to His service. For us God's great pledge of love is His gift of His

Son at Calvary. The response we must give is to be patterned on His love. He gave everything to us, not even sparing His Son nor His immortal life. We cannot do anything else but offer ourselves in sacrificial love to Him.

It is such love that enables us to obey. There are things which we are sometimes called to do which we do grudgingly. We do them because we must, not because we want to. However, when we love someone we will willingly do the same things because love makes the burden light! God's demands on His people never seem heavy when they are viewed from the foot of the Cross! And if ancient Israel did not have the Cross, they had the display of love in the deliverance from Egypt to motivate them.

But this passage tells us one more thing. The leaders of the people who had pledged themselves to the Lord saw God (vv.9–11). John tells us that no-one has ever seen God (John 1:18) and Paul says that no-one can see God and live (1 Tim 6:16). Nevertheless, though it was only the 'feet' of God that were seen by the Israelites it was a sight of great beauty and loveliness. What a contrast with the Lord who had been revealed in all His holiness in 19:18,19!

Even more remarkable was the fact that they had a meal with Him (v.11). In the ancient world no-one was invited to share a meal unless they were a very close friend. Here, however, we are told that the Israelites were invited to a meal with the Lord!

One day, we too, will see the Lord, but face to face (Rev 22:4). We, too, if we have obediently responded to the grace of God will enjoy the bridal feast of the Lamb. Yet if we have truly seen Jesus, by faith, we have already been captivated by His beauty. He is more beautiful than ten thousand and we delight to share every moment in fellowship with Him.

Questions

1. We experience God's love as we see God's love shared. In what way might God expect us to show His love to others? In practical terms, how might we show His love more obviously to those around us?

2. All Christians are in God's family with God as their father. As I reflect upon this passage do I recognise and feel this to be true? What consequences ought this recognition to have in my daily life?

Exodus 24:12–25:9

Amazing love

God reveals to His people Israel (and to us!) His amazing grace. They respond, as we should, with warmth and great generosity.

The wonderful experience of the Israelites, as described in the earlier verses of chapter 24 naturally raises certain questions. God had pledged Himself to His people as their friend. But how could the intimate and beautiful relationship of Sinai be sustained? And how could this God, who was at the same time a perfectly holy God, continue to live among a sinful people?

The remainder of the Book of Exodus is largely devoted to answering these two questions. It begins by describing the God-given plans (25:9) for the building of a 'home' for the Lord and His regulations for approaching Him. These regulations are briefly given in 25:1–9 after Moses, once again, had gone up to the mountain to meet the Lord (24:12–18). Then, in great detail the instructions are recorded (25:10–31:18) and the subsequent obedient response of the people stated (35:1–40:33). In between is the incident with the golden calf (chapters 32–33) which emphasises that the people truly were a sinful people!

Before, however, we proceed to the regulations there are several invaluable lessons taught in 24:13–25:9. We need to notice that the experience of grace opened the hearts of the people to give Him their treasures. This is no new lesson in the Book of Exodus, but it is noteworthy that it reappears here. Though the response of the people is not recorded until chapter 35 it is none the less significant that they produced 6.5 tons of precious metal for the

Tabernacle as well as fabrics which would have been very expensive materials since, in the ancient world, red, purple and blue dyes were so rare that only the wealthiest people could afford them. When one compares their generosity with the giving of most Christians it raises the question: 'How much have they experienced the grace of God, if they are so miserly?'.

The generosity of the people arose from the fact that only a few months before they had experienced an act of the Lord's delivering love which was greater than their wildest hopes. How can we, who stand in the shadow of Calvary, the gift of God which cost the life of His dear Son, respond less freely than the Israelites?

This passage does, of course, focus upon material goods. Perhaps this is because it is these things that we find most difficult to give away. However, such giving as God looks for in us is not just monetary. He looks for the best of our time, energies and gifts. We should not fail to notice this repeated emphasis in Exodus.

Questions

1. *God has lavished His treasures upon His people. As I reflect upon what Jesus did for me on the Cross do I truly realise the greatness of what God has done for me?*

2. *The amazing love of God for His children demands more than our very fullest response. As we reflect upon this passage, what might we give God more than we do?*

Exodus 25:10–22

The forgiving father

God reveals Himself as one ready to live among His people and to forgive their sins.

These verses begin the detailed description of the Tabernacle or Tent with an account of the furniture. For many readers the detail given will prove very tedious. We can get excited by the story of the Exodus itself but hardly find this material, which reads more like an architect's instructions, very thrilling! However, we need to remember that when the ancient Israelites told stories they often deliberately went into far greater detail when something very basic to their story was being told. If we are tempted not to read these chapters we need to remember this. Far from being unimportant chapters they are probably the most important part of the whole story!

The account begins with the description of the furniture. This might seem strange. We would have expected the Tent to have been described first before we were told what was to be put in it. However, the furniture was first mentioned because it was the most important part of the whole structure. Thus, we are given the design of the ark of testimony (vv.10–16); the atonement cover (vv.17–22); the table (vv.23–30) and the lampstand (vv.31–40). Strangely, the altar of incense is omitted here (compare 37:25–29).

Our concern is not to describe the various items of furniture mentioned. Of greater importance is the question 'What do these things mean?'

First of all, the purpose of the Tent and the furniture was to teach that

God intended to live with His people. In chapter 24 the leaders of the people had been invited to dine with the Lord on Sinai (v.11). It had been a quite remarkable experience of the presence of God and fellowship with Him. But was the Lord only to be present with His people on special occasions? The answer was a resounding, 'No'. His purpose was *always* to be with them. Fellowship with Him was not to be their experience only at Sinai and at other special times. He would be with them in all their wanderings 'wild and drear'. He would live with them (v.8) and ensure He stayed with them. Thus the Tabernacle was a movable structure and the Ark, which symbolised His presence, was always to have the poles by which it was moved in place (v.15).

This beautiful truth remains true today and is intended to bring us much comfort. We do not have the visible presence of the Tabernacle. But we do have the Holy Spirit in our hearts and He, likewise, guarantees the presence of God with us. We will sometimes have 'Sinai experiences' but we must not think that the Lord is not with us at other times. The God who met with His people on Sinai lived with them afterwards. In fact it could be said that it was not on Sinai but in the later wanderings that the people were to have the closer fellowship with Him because He had now come to dwell with them. The later, apparently less exciting, love of a husband and wife is, in fact, deeper than the earlier experiences of courtship. The same is often true of spiritual experience and was true of the Israelites in the desert.

The Tabernacle was also intended to remind the people of the nature of the relationship which existed between them and the Lord. This was emphasised by the name given to the chest or ark: 'the ark of testimony' (v.16). In the ark the two copies of the Ten Commandments were to be placed (see 'The Ark of the Testimony'). This was to remind the people that just as the Lord was holy, they were called to reflect His holiness (Lev 19:1–2).

The New Testament is no different (1 Pet 1:15–16, Jas 2:26). Obedience is the response of God's people which is demanded of the relationship He has entered into with them. For us, the standard of obedience is that of the Lord Jesus (John 13:34–35). He showed how God's demands are to be fulfilled.

God had delivered His people from Egypt. He had dealt with their sins through the provision of the passover lamb. Thus, the Holy God could dwell with sinners. And yet they remained people who were sinners. Their experiences on the road to Sinai had emphasised that (chapters 16–17) and the incident with the golden calf would soon make this same point again (chapters 32–33). The people were called to an obedience which they would be unable to perfectly fulfil (chapters 20–23). How then, could the God who so hated sin still remain friendly toward the people?

The answer is provided in verses 17–22 of chapter 25. Just as the Lord had provided a means by which His wrath could be averted at the time of the passover, so a similar offering would have to be repeatedly made at the atonement cover in order to deal with the continuing sinfulness of His people. This was not fully revealed to Israel until Leviticus 17. However, it is hinted at here. The atonement cover with the overshadowing cherubim was intended to symbolise the throne of God. It was the place where the Lord could be met (v.22). Yet it was an 'atonement cover' or 'mercy seat'. Thus, the assumption was made that only mercy, God's continuing mercy to sinners, secured by sacrifice, was able to preserve the relationship between the Lord and His people.

As with so much we have read in Exodus, this pointed forward to the Lord Jesus. We who are His children are called to holiness of life. It is a holiness which we can never perfectly fulfil. However, we are told that Jesus' offering of Himself in the place of sinners continues to cover our sin and guilt. John said, 'the blood of Jesus...goes on cleansing us from all sin' (1 John 1:7).

The New Testament writers never saw this as an excuse to sin. People who argued in such a way were told that they had never known the grace of God (see, especially, Rom 6). A true believer could not habitually sin. However, when they did fall into sin and repented of it they were assured of the fact that Jesus' sacrifice was able to bring them forgiveness.

We can never get beyond the need for Calvary. We continue to need the provision of God in dealing with our shortcomings. But it is only as we strive against sin and seek a righteous life that Jesus' offering for sin can avail for us.

Questions

1. God is always present with His people as their father. As we think about this truth in the light of this passage and our own experiences at the moment, how might we gain comfort and help from this fact?

2. God is present with His people as their father because of the forgiveness achieved by His son. What ought my response be to such mercy as God has shown and continues to show me?

The Ark of the Testimony

It has often been assumed that the two tablets of the law included, on the one, the first four commandments, and on the second, the last six of the Ten Commandments. Historical and archaeological research suggests that this is very unlikely. It is almost certain that each of the two tablets were identical copies of the same, complete, list of laws: one the Lord's copy and the other the people's. Thus, rather like a modern written contract, each of the parties to the agreement had a copy which emphasised their responsibilities and reminded them of their obligations to one another.

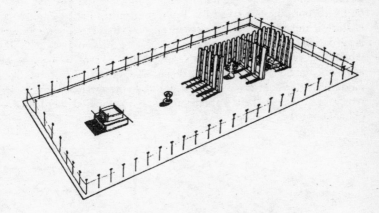

Fig. 3 Plan of the Tabernacle and court

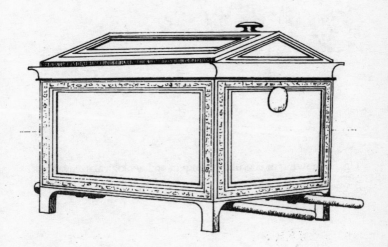

Fig. 4 The Ark and Atonement cover

Fig. 5 Drawing of cherubim found in archaeological excavations

Exodus 25:23–40

Enjoying God and His victory

God invites us to enjoy Himself not simply for what He can give us but for who He is: the source of life, joy and freedom.

The table (vv.23–30) had no particular significance in itself. All the importance lay in the 'bread of the presence' (v.30). We have already noticed that the Tabernacle was intended to provide the people with a 'continuation' of the experience at Sinai. There the leaders of the people had enjoyed a feast in the presence of the Lord. That feast had symbolised the close friendship which existed between the Lord and His people. It is the same symbolism which is found here. The friendship is continued: for God continued to 'eat' with the people. Yet the friendship was also deepened. Sinai had not led to further, occasional, invitations to a meal. Rather, the Lord was described as always at the Table in the middle of the people. Only within the context of a family is this usually true. If Sinai declared to the people that they were the friends of God, the tabernacle told them that they were His family and He was their father.

This is very important. We tend to think of God as someone available to be manipulated or, at best, as someone there when we need Him: a useful resource when we come to the end of our abilities. In all this we have a basically selfish view of God. However, this passage teaches that the relationship between God and His people is intended to be far deeper than that. He is not to be viewed as a good friend who is there to help us in trouble. He is always there. This fact does emphasise His availability: but it also reminds us of the selfless love we are expected to show Him and the responsibilities we owe Him. He is to be loved not because of what He does, but who He is. He is to be freely served: not worshipped in order that we might achieve our ambitions. There would be a great transformation in the life of God's people and their attitude to obedience and worship if this lesson were to be well learnt!

The lampstand was also intended to be symbolic. Like the other items in the Tabernacle it was intended to give an illiterate people a permanent reminder of a great spiritual truth. Two symbols seem to have been united in the lampstand. On the one hand, light would appear to have been understood as a symbol of the presence of God. Consistently, throughout the Bible the Lord is represented by fire and light. This is seen in Psalm 27:1 where, in particular, it is as the source of life and victory that the 'light' is viewed. The lampstand also seems to have symbolised the people themselves (and the seven branched candlestick is still used by the modern Jews in this sense). Thus, the Lord wished to remind the people that His presence in their midst would bring them life and victory. In the stories which follow in the Old Testament this proved to be true. When the people lived up to their high calling they enjoyed victory over all the Lord's enemies and enjoyed life to the full under His blessing.

All too often we think of freedom rather like Adam and Eve did. Freedom for them was freedom to pursue all their ambitions without any interference from God. Very quickly they learned the lesson that life apart from God was only a pale reflection of what they had once enjoyed. The Devil's counterfeit proved a very poor copy of what God had given them!

The Bible teaches very clearly that life is found, above all, in the enjoyment of God and His will for us. Yet how easily we, too, give into the temptation of the Devil.

We also need to learn that the nearer we are to God the more we will experience His victory: victory over sin and the Devil. This was the promise of the Tabernacle: it is also the promise of the indwelling Holy Spirit in us.

Questions

1. *Non Christians talk much about life and freedom. What does this passage teach about the nature and source of true life and freedom?*

2. *God's closeness to His people is to be a comfort and a challenge. In the light of this what can we learn of encouragement and rebuke from these verses?*

3. *Victory and true freedom is experienced in close fellowship with God. As I examine my own life what evidence is there that I live close to God? How might I learn to live more intimately with Him?*

Exodus 26:1–37

The majesty and nearness of God

God is here revealed as awesomely great and yet intimately near to meet the needs of His people.

These verses describe the Tent in which the furniture was housed. It was designed by the Lord (v.30) after the pattern of a travelling Arab tent but on a larger scale and with far more luxurious materials. Verses 1–14 describe the tent itself, verses 15–30 the framework over which the tent was to be fixed and verses 31–37 the curtain which was to divide the tent into two 'rooms' or compartments.

As with the furniture the tent contained symbolic elements which were intended to teach the people about God. The first great truth which it revealed was that the Lord was both a glorious God and yet One who dwelt among His people. The tent was extensively decorated with cherubim (v.1). We cannot be absolutely sure what these creatures looked like and the Bible does not give us a clear explanation of their significance. However, we can say two things about them. They are usually described as the 'bodyguard' of God himself and are always very near Him. They are also described in such a way as to emphasise that they were heavenly creatures. These facts suggest that they were intended to teach the Israelites two things. They were intended to remind God's people that the Lord was a great God, One who was over all things. Equally, they would have suggested the near presence of God Himself.

It is always necessary to hold these two truths together. Over-familiarity with the Lord was discouraged. But He was not so exalted that He was distant, unapproachable or uninterested in His people and their needs. Indeed He was present in the midst of His people. But not in such a way as would lead them to presume upon Him. Different Christian traditions seem to emphasise one or other of these great attributes of God. This is a mistake. We need both the truths and we need them together. Only then can we come to a proper understanding of Him.

However, this was not all that God revealed of Himself in the Tent. He also showed Himself to be the King of kings and the Lord of lords: in particular the Lord of His people. Thus the tent was designed on a grand scale, double the size of an ordinary tent. Then it was made of materials which were usually the privilege only of royalty. The same God who was glorious and yet present among His people was also their Lord who called forth their obedience. Only faithful obedience would enable the people to draw near to Him with confidence. We, too, can only benefit from His presence and power if we obey Him. Otherwise that presence will be known to us only as a consuming fire of judgment.

Of course, we do not have the Tabernacle. However, the Lord Jesus 'tabernacled' among us (John 1:14,18) and revealed by His life and words the character of God. And we are the temples or tabernacles of His Spirit (1 Cor 3:16). We do not have a tabernacle whose plans we must faithfully reproduce, but we do have one whose life and words are to be the model upon which to build. Moreover, our lives are to display to men and women the character of God just as the Tabernacle revealed God to the Israelites. May we be faithful!

Questions

1. *God is near but He is also great. Are we in danger of emphasising one of these truths at the expense of the other? Do we feel so cosy with God that we forget His awe-inspiring greatness or do we feel His majesty so greatly that we find it difficult to enjoy intimacy with Him? How might this passage help us to a more complete experience of God?*

2. *The Christian is God's tabernacle. Can I honestly say that my life shows forth God's glory as wonderfully as the Tabernacle did? What things tarnish my 'tabernacle'? How might I glorify God better?*

Exodus 27:1–21

Right with God

In these verses the Lord teaches us how it is possible for Him to have fellowship and enjoy friendship with sinful people such as us.

These verses complete the description of the Tabernacle and its furniture by giving the Lord's instructions to Moses for the construction of the brass altar, the court-yard boundary curtains and the night-light.

The brass altar is simply described in the verses before us. However, in 38:1 we are told its significance: it was to be the altar of the burnt offering. The burnt offering is described in detail in Leviticus 1. It was the most important of the sacrifices in the Old Testament because it was the atonement offering (Lev 1:4). Thus, a person who had sinned was expected to bring to the altar a perfect animal. Having symbolically transferred his own sins to the animal by placing his hand upon it, the offerer was then to kill it. The blood was then sprinkled on the altar and on the entrance to the Tent. This symbolised that the offerer was now protected by the blood (as in the passover) and had access again to God.

The altar would have been the first object to be seen when a worshipper entered the courtyard of the Tabernacle. This would have emphasised that the burnt offering was central to the religion of ancient Israel. It would have indicated to the worshipper the answer to the question, 'How can a holy God dwell in the midst of a sinful people?'

The significance of the horns on the altar is not obvious. However, in the ancient world (just as today) the horn was a symbol of strength and power (see Ps 18:2; 75:10). Thus, the horns may have been intended to assure the worshipper that the burnt offering had the power to bring a man or woman to God. Perhaps more likely, it would have been a reminder of the character of God: He was able to meet the needs of His people and provide a refuge from sin.

For the New Testament believer, Jesus is both the altar (Heb 13:10) and the offering. He secures our continued acceptance with God because He offered up His perfect life as an offering for the needs of His people. When we rest entirely upon Him, as the Israelites rested on the offering, we have forgiveness of sin and access to God as our friend and father; we have one who is our refuge and strength.

But there was one further significance to the burnt offering. It was completely consumed by fire in order to symbolise a life wholly dedicated to the Lord. Thus, it also pointed to the total dedication which the offerer wished to give to the Lord. Indeed, it was only under such conditions that the offering was acceptable to God. We cannot benefit from the death of Christ unless we, too, not only seek Jesus to turn away God's wrath but also willingly devote our all to Him. Only when we wish to place ourselves under His lordship can we put ourselves under the blood.

The surrounding curtain wall (vv.9–19) seems to have had little significance beyond practical necessity: it acted as a stock yard and offered some seclusion to the worshipper with its 7½ foot high wall.

However, before we pass from these verses one feature is worth a special mention. Both the altar and the fittings on the curtains were of brass. The fittings of the Tent itself were of silver and gold. This was significant. The use of precious metal throughout the area would have reminded the worshipper that he was in the courts of a king: the King of kings. However, the fact that the ordinary worshipper could not go into the tent where the more precious objects were would have also emphasised that the Lord still kept Himself at some distance from His people. There was no direct access to God for the ordinary Israelites.

How different it is today. When Jesus died the curtain which divided off God from His people was rent in two. This was quite remarkable because the curtain was of a very thick, untearable fabric. Even more amazing was the fact that it tore from the top to the bottom: curtains just do not tear that way! However, it was torn from heaven to earth to show that the way to God was now opened up for all believers! The Old Testament had not been fully able to bring men and women to God: the problem of sin remained because it was not really possible that the blood of bulls and goats could deal with sin. But Jesus dealt with sin once and for all. As a result we can enter into heaven by prayer and come right into the presence of the Lord. The Israelites could not go into the place which only symbolised God's presence, but we can enter directly into His presence. Only the High Priest could go into the Holy of Holies, where the ark and the mercy seat were, and then only once a year (Lev 17). But at every moment of every day we can approach the Lord. The writer to the Hebrews never failed to delight in this fact (see, especially, chapters 7–10). Moreover, wherever we are we have such access, whereas it was only at the Tabernacle that the Israelites had this privilege.

The last two verses (vv.20–1) of this chapter are quite delightful. For the first time the Tent is described as the 'Tent of Meeting': it was first and foremost the place where God wished to meet His people. At that tent a light was always to be alight. Even today a light is a symbol that visitors are welcome. God wanted to remind His people that He was always ready to welcome one of His children. He who kept Israel did not doze off or sleep (Ps 121:3). He was always available to meet the needs of His children!

We do not have the light, but we do have the Light (John 8:12) and His Spirit guarantees to us the blessings which Israel themselves enjoyed. Praise Him!

Questions

1. *God expects us to be ready to sacrifice all for Him. Is this true of us? What things might we be unwilling to give up for Him? Why? What encouragement does this passage give us to be ready and available for Him?*

2. *Jesus died to offer His life as payment of the penalty needed to secure our forgiveness. Am I really convinced of my need of forgiveness? Have I recognised that Jesus is the only source of my hope? Do I trust Him and Him alone for my forgiveness with God? Am I certain that He died for me?*

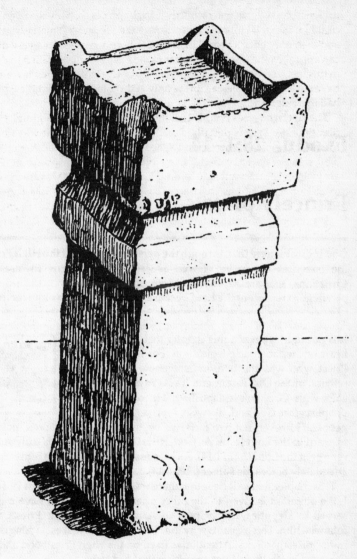

Fig. 6 Altar

Exodus 28:1–14

Princely priests

God indicates here that, through the person and work of the High Priest, the Israelites are to be viewed as princes and priests themselves. Christians, too, are royalty, children of God, and given the priestly privilege to represent the Lord because of what Jesus has done for them.

It is not until we reach this chapter that we come to the heart of the tabernacle legislation. For it was the High Priest who was the one, indispensable person in the religion of the Old Testament. It was *in him* that fellowship with God was established. He represented the people before God and, likewise, represented God to the people. However, the two facts, his being human and a sinner, pointed forward to the Lord Jesus. As God, He is the only one who is truly able to represent the Lord (John 1:14). As a sinless man He alone can represent us adequately before the Father (Heb 9:14).

This chapter makes it clear that there was really only one priest in Israel. Little attention is given to the other priests. They seem to have merely served as deputies and helpers to Aaron and the High Priests who followed him. This explains why the New Testament makes nothing of the minor priestly offices. Attention is fixed on the High Priesthood and the One who perfectly fulfilled the office: the Lord Jesus.

Nadab and Abihu (v.1) were later killed by the Lord because they disobeyed Him while engaged in their priestly duties (Lev 10:1–3). Thus, Eliezer became the High Priest when Aaron died (Num 20:28; Deut 10:16).

Six items of clothing were required for the High Priest (v.4). The Lord's instructions for them are given in detail in the chapter. Once again this emphasises the importance of what is being described. The garments are also described in a rather unusual order from the outermost to the undergarments. This is also quite deliberate and draws attention to the most important articles of the priestly clothing by mentioning them first and in greater detail. As with the construction of the Tabernacle the priestly garments were symbolic. Men and women have a tendency to think that religious clothing has a sort of magical quality. This is true even among evangelical Christians. Just listen to the believers who complain when their leader chooses not to wear the clothing that they think 'makes' him a real man of God! But even the Old Testament did not think in this way. The most important thing was that the priest was *himself* a righteous person (Ps 132:9) and the garments only symbolised God's presence among His people and His willingness to forgive and guide them: they did not secure these things.

The materials used to make the garments (v.5) were similar to those used in the construction of the Tabernacle. Thus, they were royal robes which showed that the High Priest could represent the King. Equally, they pointed to the dignity of the High Priest and the people whom he represented. They themselves were princes in the sight of the Lord of heaven! The New Testament reminds us that this also applies to us. In the Lord Jesus we are a *royal* priesthood (1 Pet 2:9). Through our High Priest we ourselves are given the dignity and privileges that only the one man had in the Old Testament. We can come before God more freely than even the High Priest could (Heb 4:14-16). We also have a duty to represent God before men. Jesus' words in Matthew 28:18-20 apply to this. We are all to go and make disciples.

Verses 6-14 describe the ephod. The writer of Exodus assumed that his readers would know the things he was describing. As a result he did not give all the details we need to understand exactly what the ephod was like. Probably it was like a waistcoat or a kilt. Perhaps it was a long sheath-like garment which came down to the knees. Whatever it looked like the most important parts of it were the shoulder straps upon which the two stones were placed which bore the names of the twelve tribes of Israel. Even today, men and women who wear uniforms often carry badges on their shoulders which show their rank. Rank carries responsibility with it. Care for junior ranks is usually part of this responsibility. This explains the importance of the two stones. The people were not allowed to enter the Tabernacle. The High Priest went in on their behalf. His responsible task was to care for the people, and, thus, to meet their needs.

It is a wonderful fact that our High Priest, the Lord Jesus, entered in heaven for us (Heb 9:24) and is there, even now, to meet our every need.

Questions

1. *Christians have the privilege of being royal! Do we feel that this is true and do we live as though we were? What a privilege to be in the princely family of the King of kings!*

2. *Christians have Jesus to care for them and meet their needs. Do I take my every need to Jesus or do I battle on until I am in a hopeless mess and really do need Him? Do I recognise that, above all, I can come to Him for forgiveness when I feel dirty and guilty?*

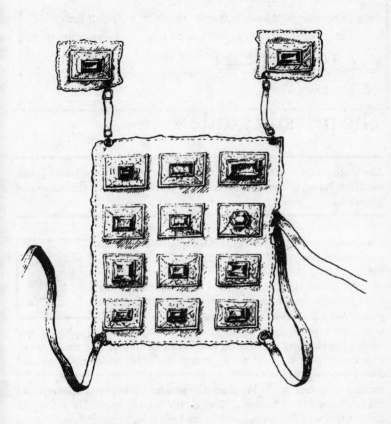

Fig. 7 Drawing of the Breastplate

Exodus 28:15–43

The priestly guide

The High Priest was to be a caring guide for the people of Israel. Jesus, our High Priest, is described in the New Testament as one who cares and guides us.

The details given in verses 15–30 make it again difficult to understand everything that is recorded here. However, the breastplate was probably a 9 inch square pouch made of similar materials to the ephod and attached to the ephod straps. On the breastplate there were 12 precious stones (which cannot be identified with any certainty) which bore the names of the 12 tribes of Israel: just like the ephod straps. In the pouch itself two stones known as Urim and Thummim were, apparently, placed. Their names meant 'the lights and perfections' and their purpose gave the name to the breastplate. It was the 'breastplate for making decisions' (v.15). We cannot be sure how these two stones enabled the Lord's will to be known and we do not need to know. The reason for this is that they fell out of use when the Lord raised up prophets to reveal His will. There was still a desire for a priest who would be able to reveal God's will much later (Ezra 2:63). But no one was raised up by God until the Lord Jesus came. He perfectly revealed God's will and has given us His Spirit to guide us safely through life. He is both our Apostle and High Priest (Heb 3:1): we should listen to Him and follow Him (Matt 17:5).

We are told one other very important fact about the breastplate: it was to be worn 'over Aaron's heart' (v.29). Thus, if the names on the shoulders pointed to the care and responsibility of the High Priest for his people, the names over the heart pointed to the love which he was expected to have for them and which the Lord had for them. The New Testament never fails to delight in the love of our High Priest. He left heaven itself to save His enemies. He did this because He loved us so much. And this is not all. He still carries our names close to His heart. In heaven, where all power is His, His heart still burns for us. What confidence this ought to give us! What a friend we have in Jesus!

The robe described in verses 31–35 was probably a long garment over which the breastplate and ephod were worn. No certainty exists as to its meaning or the significance of the pomegranates and bells which adorned the hem. It seems most likely, however, that the ornaments had a similar purpose to the tassels which the Israelites were commanded to wear on the edges of their garments (Num 15:37–41). If this is so, the pomegranates and bells may well have been intended to remind the High Priest and people that the word of God was to be faithfully obeyed. In particular, it was only when the High Priest was properly dressed that He could appear before God. It was and is Jesus' perfect faithfulness (Ps 40:8 and Heb 5:5) which pleased God and enables Him to act as our High Priest. Yet, if we are also a royal priesthood, we should seek no less a faithfulness for ourselves.

Verses 36–39 provide a description of the linen head-dress which Aaron was expected to wear. It also describes the diadem which was to be worn on the High Priest's forehead. In the ancient world it was usual to wear a covering on the head when meeting with a superior. It was a mark of respect. Aaron was expected to show respect for the Lord: a respect which was to be seen in the consecration of both him and the people whom he represented. Respect was to be evident in the obedience of the people. Thus, the diadem bore the motto, 'Holy to the Lord' (v.36). The same is to be true of us. And yet it is so sad to see the large number of people who claim to respect the Lord God yet refuse to obey Him.

However, the diadem had a greater significance. It also pointed out that the High Priest was able to mediate between the people and the Lord. Because he was 'holy to the Lord' he was able to offer up sacrifices which would take away the guilt of the people and was able to act for the people because of his holiness (v.38).

The New Testament recognised that the High Priest had not been able to perfectly do what was required of him. He was, in fact, a sinner (Heb 5:2). However, Jesus was without sin (Heb 4:15). Only He was able to really achieve what was required of the High Priest. Thus, He was able to act on our behalf and deal with the guilt of sin once and for all (Heb 10:10). Even now, He bears the emblems of His successful priesthood (Rev 1:13–16) to guarantee our continuing acceptance with God.

The brief reference to the other priests has already been mentioned. The final verses (vv.42–43) serve to emphasise the point made above. The worship of the Lord was to be done 'decently and in order' (1 Cor 14:40).

Questions

1. *Our High Priest is a tender-hearted and caring guide of His people. Do we have such confidence in Him? Or do we think Him sometimes harsh and uncaring or even unable to guide us in our needs? What ought we to learn from this passage?*

2. *As High Priest Jesus commands respect and obedience. What place does He occupy in my life? In what ways do I show disrespect for Him and fail to follow His lead?*

Exodus 29:1–46

Fellowship with God

The people of God have the privilege of living in the presence of God who lavishes His gifts upon them and delights in their obedience.

Those readers who live in parts of the world where ritual and symbolism have little importance may find this chapter difficult to understand. However, those more familiar with these things will be able to imagine the wonder, awe and mounting excitement with which Moses would have first received these instructions from the Lord!

God had delivered His people from Egypt. That was a quite marvellous thing. But His great purpose was to live with them (vv.45,46). He had provided Himself with a 'home' (chapters 25–27) and with a High Priest who would act as the 'go-between' between Himself and the people. However, not until the priest and his assistants were consecrated to their duties could He move in. Thus, this chapter marks the climax of the Exodus story so far as it describes the setting aside of the High Priest to his work. Only chapter 40 (verses 34–38) which describes the glory of God actually coming and residing with the people could outdo this chapter!

The installation of the High Priest was to begin with a wash with water (v.4). We cannot be sure whether this was by total immersion or, simply, the washing of hands and feet (30:34–38). However, the symbolism was clear. The defilement caused by sin had to be washed away (Heb 10:22). Then, and only then, could the priestly garments be put on (vv.5–9).

The New Testament uses the same symbolism. Since all believers are called to a royal priesthood they, too, need to be washed. The washing is actually done by the Lord Jesus (Titus 3:5). By His death He washes away our sin. However, the believer is to demonstrate this by being baptised (Rom 6:1–4). Then he is properly equipped to be a royal priest.

Anointing with oil is first mentioned in these verses (v.7). In 30:17–21 more details are given about the oil itself. In later years kings were anointed (1 Sam 10:1). The term was also used for the equipping of a prophet (1 Kings 19:16). Anointing seems, therefore, to have referred to God's appointment for a special task. Sometimes it was accompanied by gifts of the Spirit (1 Sam 10:6). Jesus was given the Holy Spirit in a unique way and anointed for His unique task.

As royal priests we are anointed by the Holy Spirit so that we may have the ability to live up to our calling. We are not given special clothes but we are given the fruit and graces of the Spirit. In this way we are to 'put on the Lord Jesus Christ; and to bring the knowledge of God to men and women through our holy lives (2 Cor 1:21; Gal 5:22–23; Eph 4:7; Rom 13:14; Acts 1:8).

The anointing was followed by a series of sacrificial offerings: a sin offering (vv.10–14); burnt offering (vv.15–18); peace offering (vv.19–21,31–34) and 'wave' offering (vv.22–28). The meaning of these various offerings overlaps. However, it is helpful to deal with them separately because they all add something new to the ceremonies described in these verses.

The sin offering is described more fully in Lev 4:1–5; 6:24–30. It had a similar meaning to the burnt offering. In it a perfect animal was substituted for the sinner and bore God's anger on behalf of the offerer.

The burnt offering did, of course, have an additional meaning and it is probably this which is foremost here. The sacrifice symbolised a life wholly devoted to the Lord. Thus, only the person cleansed of sin and wholly committed to the Lord could be a priest.

Jesus was without sin (Heb 4:15) and was wholly obedient to the Lord (Ps 40:6–8; Heb 10:5–7). He expects His people to be like Him. We are to have been cleansed by His blood and devoted completely to Him. Only then can we be members of the royal priesthood which is composed of all God's children.

This fact is emphasised in the third offering. A comparison between verses 31–34 and Leviticus 3:1–17 and 7:11–21 shows that the offering described here was a fellowship offering. This offering symbolised the friendship that existed between God and His people. However, it is important to notice that here it is associated with the ritual described in verse 20. There can be little doubt as to its meaning. The ear was touched to symbolise a willingness to hear the Lord, the hands were touched to indicate a willingness to do what the Lord required, the feet were anointed to bear testimony to a life completely dedicated to the Lord. Only such wholehearted devotion enabled the priest to enjoy fellowship with the Lord and no less is required of us to be His children.

Dedication was also a prominent part of the meaning of the 'wave' offering (vv.22–28). It symbolised the devotion of all the fruits of one's work to the Lord. A portion of that which was dedicated was returned to the offerer (vv.25–26) or the priests (vv.27–28). Very rarely do Christians think this way. Usually they give to the Lord what little they do not want! But they should view everything as the Lord's. They should only take from Him what they need. What a difference there would be in Christian churches if each member learnt the lesson of the wave offering!

Part of the ritual for the appointment of the priests had to be repeated every day for a week (vv.35–37). Significantly, it was the sin offering. This would have acted as a repeated reminder to the priests that they were sinners always in need of forgiveness. The same is true of the repeated burnt offering (vv.38–42). Though this particular offering was to be made for all the people it is important that it is mentioned here. Engaged daily in the work of the Tabernacle the priest could not fail to be reminded of his sin, the need for an offering for sin and God's demand of total devotion.

We must never lose sight of the cross of Jesus. Even our best is tainted with sin. Daily we are called to devote ourselves to Jesus and plead His death for sin so that our guilt might be removed.

But what a wonderful result was to follow obedience (vv.44–46): fellowship with God! The apostle John could not do anything else but rejoice in the same great fact, 'our fellowship is with the Father and with His Son, Jesus Christ' he marvelled. Are we as captivated by this great fact as we ought to be?

Questions

1. *Christians are clothed with the gifts and the graces of God. But do we wear our clothes and, even if we do, have we allowed them to become dirty and shabby? How can this happen and what should we do about it?*

2. *The privilege of obedience is fellowship with God. Do I enjoy God in this way? Could it be that I do not do so because of sin known but unrepented of? What might I do to increase my fellowship with God?*

Exodus 30:1–17

Forgiveness and fellowship

God delights to hear the prayers of His children and is always ready to make provision for the forgiveness of those sins for which they have repented.

Chapter 29 closed with the wonderful promise of fellowship with the Lord (vv.45–46). It encouraged the reader to look eagerly for the fulfilment of God's words. But what follows is a great anti-climax. Not until eleven chapters have passed will the glory of the Lord fill the Tabernacle (40:34–38) and God take up His dwelling among the people.

But a good historian (and Moses was certainly that) often delays the climax of his story. In this way he or she heightens the expectation and the tension before the exciting final scene. Moreover, several important lessons had to be taught first by Moses. It was necessary that the sinfulness of the people and especially the High Priest be shown (chapters 32–34). In this way the grace of God and the necessity of all the rituals would be established. It was also important for Moses to teach that only the detailed obedience of the people to the Lord's commands could bring God among them in such a way that it would be for their blessing (35:1–40:33)

Even before all this, however, it was necessary to record a brief collection of final instructions to the people, and, especially, the priests (30:1–31:18).

Rather strangely the altar of incense was omitted at 25:22 where a description of it might have been expected. Possibly it is included here because of its close association with the work of the priests. It was a smaller version of the brazen altar: three feet high and 18 inches square. It was placed immediately outside the curtain which led to the Holy of Holies (see 'Brazen Altar'). Psalm 141:2 and Revelation 5:8 seem to suggest that incense symbolised prayer. It was obviously the place for fellowship with the Lord (v.6). The offering of incense was also a mark of respect in the ancient world. This is hinted at in Malachi 1:11.

The overall picture presented by the altar of incense is thus clear. It was the place of fellowship with God, a fellowship marked by respect for His greatness and by access to Him in prayer. The sweetness of the incense would have indicated how gladly the Lord received the petitions of His people.

We do not have an incense altar but we do have the Lord Jesus. He is the 'incense' of our prayers. He makes them not only acceptable to the Father but also ensures they are joyfully received and answered by Him (see Heb 13:15 and Rom 8:34).

The next place of legislation is rather strange (vv.11–16) for it records a payment which had to be made to the Tabernacle whenever a census was taken. It is not at all clear why it was to take place on such an occasion. However, it obviously acted as a further reminder that the Israelites were only the people of God because He had redeemed them. Every firstborn male child and animal of the Israelites had to be redeemed (13:13) and they symbolised that the whole of the people were the firstborn of God (4:22). He had redeemed them from Egypt by means of the passover lamb. He had done so that they might live and serve Him. The payment of the shekel would have been a reminder of all this and would have taught them the debt they owed to the Lord.

Peter applies this to us in 1 Peter 1:18–19. Jesus paid our redemption price. His blood shed was the cost. As a result we are not to live as we once did. We are to live to Him.

The importance of washing in the rituals of ancient Israel was taught in 29:4. The bathing mentioned there only happened once when a new High Priest was appointed. Here (vv.17–21), we are told that whenever the priests went about their duties they had to wash their hands and feet. There was always new defilement that had to be washed away.

We, too, have been washed through the cleansing of Jesus' blood (Titus 3:5). But day by day we need to come afresh for cleansing to Him: for we shall never be free from the defilement of sin during this life. We can never get beyond a daily need of the Cross.

Questions

1. What does the emphasis upon the sacrifices and priesthood tell us about both the seriousness of sin and the mercy of God. When we share the 'good news' of Jesus with our friends, do we have a similar emphasis?

2. A Christian has the privilege of being able to freely approach God who gladly receives the prayers of His people. Is this something we experience and enjoy? What stops us from knowing this? What can we do to rejoice in the experience of free fellowship with God?

3. Daily forgiveness is available to every child of God through the Lord Jesus. Do I keep 'short accounts' with God? Do I find daily forgiveness and strength in Him? Why am I sometimes hindered from finding such forgiveness?

The Brazen Altar

Hebrews 9:4 seems to suggest that the altar of incense was within the Holy of Holies. However, since Leviticus 4:18 tells us that it was 'before the Lord', it is best to understand the reference to its being in the 'doorway' between the two parts of the tent. While it was actually outside the curtain it 'belonged' within the veil.

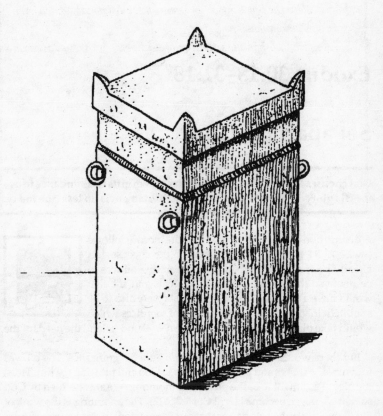

Fig. 8 Drawing of an incense altar

Exodus 30:18–31:18

Set apart for God

God chooses His children and then gives them gifts in abundance to use for His glory. What was true in the Old Testament is no less true today.

A description of the anointing oil and the incense follows (vv.22–23,34–37). The significance of the incense has already been shown (vv.1–10). The anointing oil was to be made so that all the furniture, utensils and the tent would have a pleasant smell. The priests were also to be anointed. In view of the large number of sacrifices which would take place in the courtyard we can well understand the need for the oil!

But there would seem to have been an added significance. The oil was to symbolise things and people devoted to God and pleasing to Him. Thus, the New Testament uses the picture of anointing. We are anointed by God so that we might become His (2 Cor 1:21–22). The anointing is the work of the Holy Spirit who sets us apart at our conversion. In this way our future is guaranteed (Eph 1:13–14). As royal priests we will reign with Him: because the Holy Spirit has anointed us.

It is a remarkable fact that the first person in the Bible of whom it is said, 'I have called him by name...and I have filled him with the Spirit of God' (v.2) was a workman! Indeed, his skills were the result of the Spirit's filling. Later in the Old Testament moral and spiritual qualities will also be seen as the result of the same filling. In fact all skill, strength, excellence and wisdom is from the Spirit. This is very important to notice in a day when we are inclined to think that the filling of the Spirit is limited to a tiny group of gifts. It is a remarkable testimony of our blindness when we cannot see that all gifts given to us for the benefit of God's people are the result of His filling. It is also a testimony to our folly when we place more emphasis upon gifts than moral and spiritual qualities. A careful reading of the Old Testament, beginning with Bezaleel would quickly teach us our error!

The phrase 'I have called him by name' is the first of many similar statements in the Bible. It lies behind Paul's words in Romans 8:29–30. The calling of Bezaleel led to God setting him aside for Himself and equipping him for His service.

Thus, when Paul speaks of God calling us, he means that God spoke to each one of us who are Christians and gave us a power we did not have so that, by faith (which He gave us: Eph 2:8) we have been set apart by Him and equipped by His Spirit to serve Him. He did everything that was required: from beginning to end.

What is more, He did this without giving thought to the sort of people we were or might one day become. It was a calling and anointing that was not merited in any way at all. It was by grace (Eph 2:5,8): a word which means 'unmerited'. God chose the Israelites despite the fact that they were nobodies who deserved His grace no more than any other people. He called us though we were no better than our neighbours.

This was true of Bezaleel. There is nothing to suggest that he was better than other Israelites or more likely to obey the Lord. What is true is that God called him by name.

All this is of great comfort to us. It teaches us that God is in control of everything. Paul understood this to be the result of God's grace. When we are helpless and feel our weakness we can be confident in Him (Rom 8:32–40). Moreover, what great love God has shown for us. It is not that we chose Him but that He chose us: wretched sinners though we were (see 'God's choice').

Bezaleel and Oholiab were given different gifts by the Lord. Bezaleel worked in stone, metal and wood and seems to have had skills which enabled him to make the anointing oil and incense. Oholiab was, however, responsible for the fabric work of the Tabernacle.

The New Testament teaches us that God has given us all the gifts (Eph 4:7). They vary considerably but are all necessary. They are given to us so that together the Church can be strengthened and become mature (Eph 4:7–13). Even the gifts which seem less important are valuable: sometimes more helpful than the things which we consider to be so vital (1 Cor 12:14–26). Do we use our gifts for the benefit of all the people of God? Do we proudly despise the gifts of others? Have we seen how important even our little gifts are to the work of the Lord Jesus?

The sabbath is reintroduced in verses 12–17. Perhaps all the activity in building the Tabernacle might have encouraged God's people to neglect it. But God wanted His work done in His way (a lesson we are slow to learn) and so the people were reminded to observe the sabbath. If they did not do so they were to be put to death. The severity of the penalty is explained by the fact that to disobey was to show a lack of faith in God. Disbelief made it necessary that the person be excluded from the people of God. The significance of the sabbath has already been mentioned (20:8–11; 23:10–13). However, a new fact is added here. The sabbath was a 'sign' (v.12) intended to keep the people in the knowledge of God. We also have signs which have been given to us. In particular, baptism and the Lord's Table are signs which we are intended to observe so that our faith in God is nourished. All too often, Christians are disobedient in these matters. They refuse to be baptised or rarely attend the Lord's Table. The danger that faces them is the same as that which faced the disobedient Israelites. They will one day have to face God's judgment.

The last verse in this section (v.18) reminds us that God gave Moses the two copies of the Ten Commandments. They were unique among all the words which God had spoken because they, alone, were written by God Himself. This emphasised how important it was that they were obeyed.

These great principles are just as relevant to us as they ever were to Israel. However, we have more than the Ten Commandments. When God wished to reveal His will to us He sent us His Son. We are, above all, called to listen and obey Him. The Israelites were to show that they really were God's children by responding to His love in obedience to the Ten Commandments. We can only prove that we have received the grace of God when our lives show our faithfulness to Jesus.

Questions

1. *What does this passage teach us about how we ought to view and use the gifts that God has given us?*

2. *Every believer has the Holy Spirit living inside them. Since this is so, what gifts has the Holy Spirit given me or how might I find out what gifts I have?*

3. *The God of the Bible is the God of grace. As I reflect upon this passage what sort of response should I offer to God for His amazing grace toward me?*

God's choice

What we have said here is not intended to deny our responsibility to believe the Christian message. We are commanded to believe (Acts 17:20) and are warned of the consequences of rejection of God (Heb 12:25). We are told that God does not want anyone to perish, but rather desires that everyone come to repentance (1 Pet 3:9).

In fact we are faced with a mystery. God is the author of our salvation but we are responsible for rejecting Him. This is impossible for human minds to understand. Yet it does help answer the question, 'Why did I believe and not others?'.

Some who have heard the Christian message are nicer people than we are and have a clearer understanding of the message of the Bible. But we have believed and they have not! Why did we seek God and not them? To many Christians, the only answer is that God Himself did it!

Exodus 32:1–19

Improving on God's way

We have a tendency to come up with religions which we consider superior to that which God Himself has revealed. Such may offer cheap, undemanding grace and the blessing of God but are hated by Him!

For forty days Moses was instructed by the Lord on the mountain (24:18). Chapters 25–31 provide a summary of what he was taught. Meanwhile, the people were left alone at the foot of Sinai. These verses begin by recounting what had taken place while Moses was away.

It is unlikely that the Israelites would have been tempted to desert the Lord so soon after leaving Egypt. However, Moses had symbolised God's presence with them and now he was gone. A substitute was required. So the people asked Aaron to 'make us God' (v.1): a symbol of the Lord's presence (see 'God or gods').

When men and women depart from the revelation of God they end up with a religion which is perversion. This was true when Aaron made the golden bull. Instead of the ark, the atonement cover, the cherubim and the tables of the law was a bull.

A bull was a symbol of brute strength and power as well as fertility. The children of Israel thus pictured God as someone who might fulfil their personal and basically selfish ambitions. In marked contrast was the Lord who had revealed Himself to Moses. He was a holy God who hated sin but who wished to enjoy the friendship of His people. He was a God who demanded a holy life of His followers. Aaron showed how inadequate his view of God was. Sin offerings and fellowship offerings were made (v.6) but an orgy then followed. For him the offerings were there to manipulate God while men and women could continue in their sinful ways. His was a cheap religion which demanded nothing of its followers.

This sort of religion has always appealed to religious people because it is basically selfish. It offers cheap, undemanding grace and the blessing of God. It offers forgiveness but does not demand repentance. What more could we want!

But such a religion is hated by God. It is not religion at all (v.7). Gradually, in this section of Exodus the nature of true religion is revealed in contrast to the counterfeit offered by Aaron.

First God told Moses that the people who had made the bull were bull-necked (v.9)! They were like a bull who could not be controlled by a bridle. As a result they were constantly fighting against His purpose for them and He was extremely angry with them (v.10). God was ready to reject them and to fulfil His plans through Moses (v.11).

This is the truth about false religion. Whatever it offers it cannot provide. God does not offer friendship to rebels. Yet how many of us have a Christianity that is almost identical to the religion of Aaron. How few believers seem to live a life of daily repentance from sin and devoted service to the Lord.

In Mark 1:12 (and see Matt 4:1–11; Luke 4:1–13) Jesus was driven into the wilderness to be tempted by the Devil. The temptation was to receive all the glory with none of the cost (Matt 4:8,9; Luke 4:5–7). But if Jesus had agreed He would never have been able to act as our mediator and saviour. Though it was the Lord who spoke to Moses (v.10) the test was the same. God had promised that He would fulfil His purposes for the salvation of mankind through a descendant of Judah (Gen 49:10). God may have made a great nation of Moses but if He did this the Saviour of the world could never come. And yet what a temptation it must have been to Moses. He had already discovered that being the leader of God's people was no easy task (5:20–21; 6:9; 16:1–17:7). However, he was used to leading silly sheep and (unlike the Moses of earlier years) he held the glory of God and the blessing of the people as greater than any personal ambitions.

In this Moses showed the same attitude as Jesus who endured the Cross for the sake of His people. We, too, are expected to conduct ourselves in the same way. And yet how many Christians, and especially Christian leaders, know the temptation to take the easy path when faced with the cost of following Jesus.

It is to Moses' credit that he does not seem to have considered what God offered him. Immediately, he pleaded with God on behalf of the people (vv.11–13). He did not excuse the people's sin as we might have been inclined to do (see Aaron's response in verse 22). Whereas the Lord had spoken of 'your people' (v.7) Moses pleaded the fact that they were the Lord's (v.11). He argued on the basis of the glory of God (v.12) and, above all, from His promises (v.13).

It is one of the greatest temptations of Christian leaders to seek their own glory rather than the Lord's. This was the problem with Diotrophes who loved to be first (3 John 9). Few are like John the Baptist who said, 'He must become greater; I must become less' (John 3:30). Moses had the same attitude. He sought the glory of God above his own peace.

Moses' prayer is typical of the sort of prayer which the Lord hears. But though God relented from bringing His judgment upon the people (v.14) the full relationship which He had planned to exist between Himself and them was still broken. This is seen by Moses' reaction when he reached the camp of the Israelites (v.19). He broke the two copies of the covenant. Obviously he did this when faced with the full horror of what God had previously told him. However, he also did so because the covenant which the Lord had revealed to him on the mountain lay in ruins with the people's disobedience. Thus, though God had suspended His judgment they remained His enemies.

Questions

1. *What lessons does this passage have for us when faced with the claims of other religions? Are there lots of different ways to God?*

2. *God is the God who has revealed Himself, not a God who human beings have invented. As we reflect upon this passage, is our understanding of God based upon what is taught in the Bible or have we added, or taken away, from its picture of Him? What does this passage teach us about what God is really like? How does this challenge ideas we might have concerning Him?*

3. *True religion is to enjoy the presence of God and serve Him wholeheartedly. To what extent does my faith correspond with that of Moses? Where do I differ from him? What do I need to learn from this passage?*

God or gods

The word for gods and the word for God is identical in the Bible. Thus, in this passage the people could be asking for gods to replace the Lord.

However, since Aaron told them to prepare to celebrate a festival to the Lord (v.5) it is more likely that a symbol of God was sought.

Later, in Canaan, a bull was used, not as a symbol of a god himself but a representation of his throne. This is probably what we should understand by the golden bull in Exodus.

The incident here is often known as that of the 'golden calf'. In fact 'bull' is better. The word actually used is of a young bull at the height of its strength and power.

All this suggests that Israel were asking for a throne-emblem which would symbolise the presence of the Lord. Their sin was not idolatry but, as we see, building a religion which was not based upon what God had revealed.

Fig. 9 Canaanite Baal

Exodus 32:20–33:17

Infirmity in place of sin and blessing in place of forgiveness?

This passage warns us that there is a danger that we seek a religion which offers blessing and minimises the problems caused by sin rather than follow God's way and recognise sin for the offence it is and, yet, find delight in His provision of forgiveness.

The second action of Moses when he returned was to destroy the image and make the people drink the powdered gold (v.20). Presumably this would have shown the people the powerlessness of the religion which they had invented. It may also have been an ordeal (see Num 5:5–31) by which, in some way which is not recorded for us, the ringleaders were identified by the Lord. This may explain the slaughter of verses 25–29.

By these actions Moses showed a totally different attitude to sin than that of his brother (vv.21–24). Aaron had given in to the weakness of the people. Moses called that weakness sin! Just like Adam and Eve before him (and like countless millions since!) Aaron also tried to put the blame somewhere else. He first blamed the people (v.22) and then the furnace!

We can laugh at Aaron. But when we do so we are actually laughing at ourselves. For we are no different. Even Christian believers refuse to face up to the full horror of their disobedience. They are always ready to blame friends, family, society, circumstances, anything: providing that they can escape the full blame and judgment for rebelling against God. However,

Moses realised that in the end we cannot escape the charge of sin: for that is what it really is.

The full extent of the rebellion against the Lord is seen in verse 25. In tactful terms a naked riot of sexual frenzy is described (see also v.6). This was typical of the religion of Canaan. Several of God's laws had already shown His hatred of sexual sins (20:14,26; 22:16,19; 28:42). However, it is often the demands the Lord puts upon our sex lives that are the first that we ignore. Like Israel we like to think that it does not matter or, as they did, find some good religious reason to excuse our conduct. For them it was obvious that sexual licence was to be encouraged so that God could be reminded that they needed fertile crops and herds. We do not use the same arguments but the result is the same: we disobey the Lord.

It is not easy to understand verses 26–31 (see 'A variety of Versions'). The details are obscure. However, Moses called for those who were on the Lord's side to stand up for Him and wage war against sin. This proved costly (vv.27,29) for some of the nearest relatives of those who responded to the Lord were the ringleaders of the rebellion. Nevertheless, their faithfulness to their difficult task won the approval of the Lord (v.29). In a world in which sin invites us on every side the battle against sin is always difficult and costly. However, in the end it achieves the only worthwhile prize in this life: the blessing of God.

To some Moses' action might seem harsh. But men are usually far more violent in putting down rebellion. Three thousand was a small proportion of the people. The action was a merciful one which was intended to point out to the people the seriousness of their condition.

This fact was also emphasised by Moses' words on the following day (v.30). They had committed a 'great sin'. However, it is at this point that the greatness of Moses shines through. God had withdrawn the threatened judgment (v.14) in response to his prayer. But Moses' desire for the people was far greater than that. His wish was that they might be forgiven and that the Lord's purpose of dwelling with His people be fulfilled. He did not minimise their folly before the Lord (v.31) but he pleaded with God for forgiveness: even if he had to lose his own eternal security! He would willingly have sacrificed his own life to the wrath of God, if only the Lord would forgive the people (v.32, see also Rom 9:3).

The Lord refused Moses' offer (v.33) for none could die in the place of others until the sinless Saviour died. The sinners had to face God's wrath (v.35). However, God did make one concession to Moses. The promise of the land (see vv.13,34) was restored to the people. But no longer would the Lord go up with them. He would send an angel. This angel was not the same as the angel of the Lord (see 3:15–16) for that angel was a symbol of God's presence. And it was the Lord's presence which was still forbidden to the people (33:3).

For many of us this might have seemed the ideal solution to our religious needs. God was offering Moses all the blessings which the people had sought in their 'bull-god' but without the uneasiness of the presence of God who hated and judged sin. Most of us would volunteer to be members of this sort of religion. The people were expelled from Sinai, where the Lord was present, but sent to the land (33:1–3).

However, the people had come to a sufficient understanding and repentance that this was not enough for them (v.4). The Lord's response begins in verse 5. He warned them exactly what having God in their midst could mean (v.5a and see Amos 3:2). However, whereas Moses himself could not achieve their forgiveness and reconciliation, God hinted that by their own repentance it might prove possible. Then he tested their sincerity by asking for their treasures (vv.5,6).

But the Lord made it clear that forgiveness and reconciliation were no easy thing for Him to give. Indeed, as the New Testament teaches us, it could not be finally achieved without the Lord offering up His Son for sin. So no immediate response was given to the people's desire.

In the meanwhile, Moses set up a tent. The purpose of the tent was similar to that of the Tabernacle. It was the meeting place between God and man (vv.9,10). However, it was outside the camp, whereas the Tabernacle would be right in the centre (Num 3). Also the presence of God was only given to Moses (v.9) when he went to the tent. The people had to keep their distance (vv.8,10).

Finally, God answered the desires of the people and the request of Moses for reconciliation (v.14). It is not, however, clear what Moses' final prayer was (vv.12–13). Probably we should understand his words in this way. God had promised Moses that he would enjoy His presence. This is what to 'know my name' seems to mean. On the other hand God had only promised to send an un-named angel together with Moses and the people so that they might enter the land of Canaan. Moses seized on this. If the Lord was to truly go with him (and he did not want anything else: v.15) then an un-named angel was not enough for the people. The people could have nothing less than Moses himself enjoyed! Unless this were true then the people would be no different from any other people fleeing from slavery (v.16).

God answered Moses' bold prayer (vv.14,17) for his sake. Thus does the Lord forgive and reconcile us because of the prayers of the Lord Jesus.

Questions

1. *What does this passage emphasise as being at the very centre of the Christian message? Is it central in our teaching and sharing?*

2. *Sin is sin! What sort of excuses do we come up with to avoid facing the fact that there are sins in our lives? Are we really so different from Aaron?*

3. *True religion alone brings forgiveness. Am I more interested in the fun and the blessing of Christianity or do I want to know my sins forgiven and live as a child of God? Is my religion ultimately empty or do I have the assurance of sins forgiven and fellowship with God?*

A variety of Versions

The things that are described in chapters 33 and 34 are so wonderful and almost impossible to put into words that it is difficult to know what exactly is being said and described. This explains why the different versions of the Bible vary in what they say. Moses was trying to describe the indescribable. How much more difficult is it for those who try to translate our Bible to understand and put into words what Moses found difficult to say. In these pages we have tried to suggest what probably happened.

Exodus 33:18–34:7

This is your God

This passage describes more fully than almost any other part of Scripture the greatness, glory and majesty of God...our God!

There are times in our Christian lives when we are faced with a new challenging situation. All that we have believed and known of God in the past is not enough to enable us to confidently go on in faith. We need some new understanding of the Lord. Moses had the same experience. The Lord had promised to forgive and reconcile His people to Himself and to go with them to the land of Canaan. But could Moses be sure of this? What would happen if the people let the Lord down again? Faced with these questions Moses did not seek a sign from the Lord (see p. 34). What He did ask for was a fuller knowledge of God (v.18). Moses asked to see God. This, he was told was not possible (see also Judg 6:22; 13:22; Is 6:5 and 1 Tim 6:16). Sinful men cannot see God and live. However, the Lord did promise Moses the knowledge which he needed (vv.19–23).

Chapter 34:1–28 describes the Lord's response to Moses' two requests. First of all God took the necessary steps to re-establish His special relationship with the Israelites (v.2). Verses 2–3 repeat the demands of the Lord when the covenant was first made (19:10–13,20). The terms of the relationship were then rewritten (vv.1,28).

Sometimes it is suggested that the second copies of the Ten Commandments were written by Moses whereas the original copies were written by God. This is unlikely. Verse 1 tells us that both Moses and the Lord wrote the tablets! This is probably what took place on the first occasion as well. God so supervised the writing of the words that they could properly be called His. This is, of course, true of all the Bible. However, it is especially mentioned here to teach the great significance of these words.

In verses 4–7 we have the Lord's response to Moses' second request. He gave to Moses a new revelation of Himself. It is impossible to know exactly what happened and what Moses saw (vv.19–23; 34:4–7). We should not be troubled by this because its importance to Moses and to us is made clear. God proclaimed His name, 'the Lord' (v.5). He revealed more fully to Moses what His name meant. Eight separate things were said to Moses.

(1) 'The Lord, the Lord' The name of God was probably repeated to imply the same truth as was later taught by speaking of God as the 'alpha and the omega' (Rev 1:8; 22:13). The whole history of Israel had begun, continued and existed until the present moment because of the unchanging power of the Lord (see also Heb 13:8). This is a truth which believers seem so slow in learning. They tremble before the future or even in their present distress. But they forget that the Lord has proved to them time and again His unchanging power to meet them in their needs. And he does not change.

(2) 'the compassionate and gracious God' The word 'compassionate' comes from a word which describes the feeling of pity which a mother has for her helpless baby (Ps 103:13). It suggests that the Lord can *feel* our needs. The New Testament tells us that this is especially true since the Son became a man and shared our experiences (Heb 4:15). The word 'gracious' means kindness to those who have no right to expect it. It was seen in the Good Samaritan and is perfectly expressed by Paul in Romans 5:8, 'God shows his love toward us in that while we were yet sinners Christ died for us'. Again and again Christians feel that they are plunged into situations that no one understands. As they mature as believers they become increasingly conscious of their sinfulness and weakness. It is a great comfort in such situations to be reminded that the Lord is compassionate and gracious.

(3) 'slow to anger' How much Moses needed to hear these words! The people were so weak and liable to sin. What a tremendous comfort these words must have been. Men sometimes interpret God's slowness in punishing sin as a sign of weakness or as a good reason for not taking His wrath seriously. As believers we must not make the same mistake. And yet what a blessing to know that though we do fail God will deal mercifully with us when we turn again to Him. What a mercy that He gives us time to repent.

(4) 'abounding in love and faithfulness' 'Love' is faithfulness to promises, especially promises made within a covenant. 'Faithfulness' means utterly trustworthy. God had made some almost unbelievable promises to Moses. The listing of the names of the inhabitants both here and elsewhere must have been enough to make the people tremble (see Num 13:26–33 for a later but similar reaction). It was in this situation that God assured Moses that He kept His promises with complete faithfulness. For the Christian there are many promises made to us that are so great that we find them difficult to believe. We, too, must never forget, though we sometimes tremble, that God is faithful and trustworthy.

(5) 'maintaining love to thousands' The thought here is that God keeps faith generation after generation. Often this has proved to be literally true. Many Christians are the children of godly parents, grandparents and even great-grandparents. But the Lord's words also suggest that He does not keep changing His plans or allow a small upset to spoil a relationship. Friends sometimes do separate: frequently for the silliest reasons. The Lord assured Moses that He would not be like that with Israel, even though they sometimes sorely provoked Him. What a blessing it is that we also have the same God.

(6) 'forgiving wickedness, rebellion and sin' Wickedness refers to the natural tendency to sin in men and women which has characterised everyone, except Jesus, since Adam and Eve fell into sin. Rebellion is the act which breaks God's revealed purpose for men. Sin is the failure to live up to His standards. Together the words refer to sin in all its different forms. God promised Moses to forgive any and every sin! Sometimes Christians and others think that they have acted in such a way as makes it impossible for God to ever forgive them. They know that Jesus died for sin. But they somehow feel that what they have done is too bad for even Him to forgive them. These words to Moses must have been a great consolation. Israel had committed a dreadful sin. But there was forgiveness for them: just as there is, then, for us.

(7) 'Yet He does not leave the guilty unpunished' This may seem to contradict what the Lord had just said. But this is not true.

God forgives every repentant sinner and deals with their guilt. In the Old Testament He provided the sin and burnt offerings. In the New Testament He provided His own Son to suffer and bear the guilt of repentant sinners.

(8) 'He punishes the children...to the fourth generation'

The first thing to notice here is that God does not deal as severely with the wicked as we might have expected. If He maintains His love to thousands of generations we might expect that His judgment would be of a similar order. But in fact it is far, far less. Truly, He is gracious and compassionate even to sinners.

Nevertheless we do need to remember that our sin affects others and often leads them into sin. We must take seriously the warning that our sin can lead others to Hell.

This great revelation of God to Moses became the foundation upon which the religion of Israel was built. Time and time again these words are repeated (Num 14:18; 2 Chron 30:9; Neh 9:17; Pss 86:15; 103:8; 108:4; 111:4; 116:5; 145:8; Joel 2:13). We are to build on them too. One thing alone is missing. We see the glory of God in the face of Christ Jesus (2 Cor 4:6). As we look at Him all these things are perfectly revealed to us. Thus, when Christians sometimes regret that they have not had an experience like Moses had they are wrong. What greater glory could the Lord have displayed to us than the glory He has revealed in His Son? We need to spend our time meditating upon Him.

Questions

1. *How different is this picture of God from the 'popular' version that so many non Christians hold! What might we do to correct this misconception?*

2. *God is a wonderful God indeed! What can we learn from Moses' experience which might challenge us and encourage us to go on to maturity by faith in Him?*

3. *God never fails to meet His children in their needs. As I reflect upon Moses' experience of the faithfulness of God and on my own past experience, what reassurance do I have that God will always help me when I need Him?*

Exodus 34:8–35

Reflecting God's glory

Nearness to God leads to our reflecting His glory. What was true of Moses is to be true, in some measure, of us too!

The remarkable experience of Moses described in verses 1–7 is followed by his confession of the people's sin (vv.8,9). There is, however, one difference from 32:31. There Moses prayed for others. Now he included himself among the sinners. Great man though he was he knew that he was no different from those who had sinned so
openly. This is the mark of a truly spiritual person. Moses knew that the Lord looks on the heart. He knew that sin dwelt in his own heart. There was both the natural tendency to turn away from God and a failure to live up to the Lord's standards even in him. The Apostle Paul could think of himself as the 'least of all the saints' (Eph 3:8). The longer a Christian has been a Christian the more certain he or she is that the same is true of them. They can only plead the mercy of God for forgiveness and reconciliation (v.9).

God confirmed that He would receive the people (vv.10–11) but, once again, He reminded Moses that He expected obedience of those who had received His forgiveness. Verses 10–28 do not add anything that is new. They were intended to summarise the demands which God made in 20:1–23:19. In particular, laws which were intended to keep Israel distinct from the ungodly nations around them were emphasised. This was most important. The incident with the golden bull had already shown the danger of adopting the religious ideas of the Canaanite peoples. Laws which would prevent this from ever happening again if the people obeyed were, therefore, repeated.

Paul told the Roman Christians to 'be renewed by your minds' (Rom 12:2). He was convinced that if the believers began to think like the Lord they would be able to approve the right course of action and recognise and avoid evil. In this way they would remain distinct from the unbelievers and be a powerful witness to them. The fact that Christians so rarely seem any different from unbelieving people shows that they have taken neither Moses nor Paul seriously.

It is a fact that when two people have known one another for a long period of time they begin to think and speak and even look like one another! The Bible knows that this is true and tells us that this is true when we have been with the Lord. This was illustrated by the experience of Moses (vv.29–35). The glory of God which had been his experience for 40 days could be seen, reflected in his face. We are not told why Moses put a veil over his face. However, the Apostle Paul suggested that it was because Moses did not want the people to see the glory fade. Since the people were anxious for things which they could see to support their faith (see 32:1) God probably commanded Moses to put on the veil in order that the people would not judge him on the basis of whether his face shone or not. In the passage in 2 Corinthians 3 where Paul speaks about the veil, he tells us that there is a remarkable difference between the experience of Moses and our own experience. After a while the glory on Moses' face began to fade. But the glory which comes from knowing Jesus lasts. Our experience, if we truly know Him is not that the glory fades. It rather increases as day by day we are gradually transformed into the likeness of Jesus (2 Cor 3:7–18). May it be true of us as we look ever more intently at Him.

Questions

1. *A mature Christian is more and more aware of sin in his or her life. Are we sufficiently conscious that we remain sinners with the seeds of sin still deep in our hearts?*

2. *A truly spiritual person thinks God's thought after Him and begins to reflect His glory. What do I do, or might I do, to ensure, so far as is possible, that I think the same way as God Himself does?*

Exodus 35:1–40:38

Heaven on Earth!

God comes down to live in the midst of His faithful and obedient people.

With the steady plod of a man or woman returning home at the end of a busy day's work, these chapters describe the faithfulness of the people to the commands which God had earlier given to Moses. This is taught in two different ways. First of all the earlier instructions are repeated almost word for word as the Israelites obey them. Thus:

35:1–3	repeats	31:12–17
35:4–9	"	25:1–9
35:30; 36:1	"	31:1–11
36:8–38	"	26:1–37
37:1–29	"	25:10–39; 30:1–5,23–35
38:1–20	"	27:1–19; 30:18
39:1–31	"	28:1–43

In addition to this the last two chapters each include a sevenfold repetition of the words 'as the Lord commanded Moses' (39:1,7,21,26,29,31,32 and 40:19,21,23,25,27,29,32). Since the number seven is often used to indicate perfection in the Bible this is probably a deliberate and repeated statement of the perfect obedience of the people.

This obedience was undertaken willingly. This is stressed in the early chapters (35:5,21,22,26,29; 36:3). Moreover, as these chapters are read it is clear that the perfect and willing obedience of the people brought them great joy. Later in the Old Testament the same truth is found very clearly taught in the books of Chronicles. It is a lesson we are slow to learn. Yet it remains true that the really happy person is the one who willingly and perfectly obeys the Lord.

The willingness of the people was seen in the way that they provided for the materials of the Tabernacle. Their response was amazing. Chapter 38:21–31 tells us that they brought one ton of gold, four tons of silver and three tons of copper. Indeed they brought so much that they had to be stopped (36:7)! But it was not just the materials which they brought to the Lord. They also devoted their time and their talents to the Lord (35:25; 36:2,4,8 etc.). Everyone seemed to be involved (35:23,24,25,27) under the leadership of Bezaleel and Oholiab.

In all this the Israelites are an example and a challenge to us. The New Testament church, at its best, showed exactly the same attitude (2 Cor 8: 1–5; Phil 4:14,19; Eph 4:16). Yet how few churches reflect the same picture of delight and wholehearted obedience among all the people of God. What a rebuke this is to us. We fail with all our advantages, where the Israelites were faithful.

Chapter 39:32–43 seems to echo Genesis 1:1–2:4. This is probably deliberate. The people of God were the new creation of God (see 2 Cor 5: 17). In them the original purpose of God for the world was to be displayed.

Nothing then remained to be done, except that the Lord, whose continual presence and fellowship had been lost by Adam and Eve (Gen 3: 22–24), returns and dwells with His people. This is recorded in the last, thrilling verses of Exodus. The dwelling place of God was once again with man!

And yet . . . no one can read the book of Exodus without a great sense of anti-climax. Though the Lord was, once again, in the midst of His people it was not characterised by that intimate fellowship between God and man which had been the experience of Adam and Eve. Moreover, though the people had escaped from Egypt and its gods those gods still seemed to exercise a fatal power over the people. They were still, all too often, ready to sin and desert the Lord. And, though Israel was redeemed, the rest of the world still lay under the curse of God.

But amid this sense of anti-climax (which is only heightened in the burdensome rituals of Leviticus and the frequent disobedience of the people in Numbers) there is also a renewed sense of anticipation. Time and again the book of Exodus points forward. It has emphasised that the answers it gives to mankind's needs are only temporary and provisional.

God's final answer to man's need is still awaited.

Gradually, in the remaining books of the Old Testament, this anticipation becomes greater and greater. New promises are added and fresh understanding given of man's predicament and God's plans.

Then . . . we are told of an angel who appeared to a poor carpenter: a member of a despised nation and town. To him the angel said 'Joseph, son of David, do not be afraid to take Mary home as your wife . . . She will give birth to a son, and you are to give Him the name Jesus, because He will save His people from their sins' (Matt 1: 20–21). At last, the Saviour of the world had come!

Thus, the New Testament never fails to rejoice in one who was greater than Moses (Heb 3); Aaron and the priesthood (Heb 7–10); who offered a greater sacrifice (Heb 10) and was Himself the altar, the incense etc. and one day will return, accompanied with the words, 'Now the dwelling place of God is with man, and he will live with them. They will be His people, and God Himself will be with them and be their God' (Rev 21:3).

'Maranatha, so come Lord Jesus' (1 Cor 16:22).

Questions

1. *God expects His people to be a community committed to one another. Is our view of the church big enough to contain God's vision? Do we seek, so far as we are able to, to help our own church realise God's plan for it? What might we practically do to ensure that His plan is not frustrated by us?*

2. *Jesus is the hope of the world! How do my attitudes, actions and expectations square up to the hope which He has brought into the world?*

Appendix:

For further reading

Exodus is not well served by the commentators. For devotional reading Matthew Henry remains largely unchallenged, though his interpretation needs to be checked against more recent expositions.

The major scholarly commentary is probably J.I. Durham, *Exodus*, Word Bible Commentary, Word, 1987. This offers a basically conservative and scholarly explanation of the book. Older, more conservative and generally useful is W.H. Gispen, *Exodus*, Bible Students Commentary, Zondervan, 1982 (English translation of the Dutch). Other important works are more liberal in their approach; e.g. J.P. Hyatt, *Exodus*, New Century Bible, Marshalls, 1971; B.S. Childs, *Exodus*, SCM Old Testament Library, 1974; G.A.F. Knight, *Theology as Narration*, Handsel Press, 1976.

Most readers of this book will probably look no further, however, than Alan Cole, *Exodus*, Tyndale Old Testament Commentary, IVP, 1973. It is, however, rather thin on content. The Daily Study Bible on Exodus by H.L. Ellison, St Andrew Press, 1982 is a useful supplement.

J.J. Davis, *Moses and the Gods of Egypt*, Baker offers good background material.